Best Wishes and God Bless Jim

Pretty Smart For A Girl

Jewell E. Myers May

Jewell E. Myers May

WestBow
PRESS
A DIVISION OF THOMAS NELSON

WestBow Press books may be ordered through booksellers or by contacting:

WestBow Press
A Division of Thomas Nelson
1663 Liberty Drive
Bloomington, IN 47403
www.westbowpress.com
1-(866) 928-1240

Because of the dynamic nature of the Internet, any Web addresses or
links contained in this book may have changed since publication and
may no longer be valid. The views expressed in this work are solely those
of the author and do not necessarily reflect the views of the publisher,
and the publisher hereby disclaims any responsibility for them.

ISBN: 978-1-4497-0606-7 (sc)
ISBN: 978-1-4497-0607-4 (e)

Library of Congress Control Number: 2010937808

Printed in the United States of America

WestBow Press rev. date: 10/28/2010

In loving memory of Mamma, Daddy and Dennis

For Harold

Preface

"Down Boy"

Those are the words my brain has heard most of my life. My brain has been trained to not expand and think of thought-provoking things. Being born a girl and into a family that was accustomed to keeping the female members in a subservient stance it was difficult to determine if an intelligence was there.

When I was very young I overheard my father tell a neighbor, "She is pretty smart for a girl." I remember thinking "What does being a girl have to do with it?" The slight was remembered and my girl's brain had no difficulty recalling it time and time again through the ensuing years.

My brain was in a constant tug-of-war. It was eager to learn and this little girl learned to read and sew and do all the girly things and at the same time feeling that it was not to verbally demonstrate intelligence.

When I learned something exciting in school I would rush home and tell my parents what I learned and my father would say, "Don't you know better than to believe everything that damn teacher tells you?" It didn't take long for me to keep all the knowledge to myself and then in time I learned not to demonstrate it even if I felt it was appropriate. There were times when I could hardly contain myself. It was indeed hard to keep quiet when every fiber of my body was disagreeing with the views being discussed.

I learned that it didn't take much for me to outwit both my parents. Occasionally when the time was right I would interject a statement which would stop Dad in mid statement and he would sit and think and the expression "That's right" would appear on his face.

Please don't misunderstand me regarding my parent's intelligence. They were both highly intelligent but they were unlearned. I worked for a man one time who liked the phrase, "He may be stupid but he isn't dumb." It took me a long time to figure out what he meant. Neither of my parents completed eighth grade. It never occurred to me how much Dad regretted his being unable to complete school.

It must have been in 1940 when the census taker came around to our farm and standing in the barnyard asking his usual questions including "how much education do you have?" When Dad replied that he only went through the seventh grade he looked at the ground.

Mom got as far as the seventh grade and dropped out since she had to miss so much school to run the house while my grandmother was busy being sick. (That lady was sick all her life. My grandfather moved the family to Arizona for her health and she was sick all the time they were there. After four years in the dry climate they returned to the Central U. S. where she continued to nurse her aches and pains until she died at the ripe old age of 92.)

My parents were angry people and always worried about their plight in life. These two factors require much strength and energy thus depleting the ability to concentrate and expound signs of intelligence.

As the years progressed and I entered high school, I read many books and newspapers and continued to quietly expand my knowledge. It was hard for me to understand why society expected me to marry, as all good girls did, and have children and run a home even if they would really rather be doing something else.

My teachers are to be commended, especially my home economics teachers. They taught us the importance of running the home in a scientific mode and the importance of time management. It became clear to me that operating a home was indeed rewarding, however, I continued to feel that it wasn't for me.

However, when I met my future husband I took a wholesome interest in homemaking. We married and during the next decade or so we had six children. It has been obvious during the years of mothering and 125% homemaking that I relied heavily on my skills learned in home economics. It is doubtful I would have succeeded without that training. Each time a new baby was brought home from the hospital I would sit down and do a schedule to determine how I could fit all the duties into my 24-hour day.

During those years of intense homemaking I never quite found time to read and further my learning. Television came along and I enjoyed the educational programs but the entertainment programs were such silly nonsense that I felt guilty when I abandoned my duties to watch it.

The children grew up, as children do, and now have families of their own and it is possible for me to harbor my hobbies. I am involved in many things, one of which is writing my life's story. I had the opportunity to take a workshop on memoir writing in St. Augustine, Florida. Some of my articles were published in our church monthly there.

In later years, I have been fortunate enough to have some of my work also published in professional magazines and newspapers, which has been a boost to my ego and self-esteem. My Dad's opinion of me has been enhanced time and time again, and I guess I am pretty smart even though I am a girl.

Acknowledgements:

Many thanks go to my family and friends for believing in me and the members of the "Southern Sisters" book club for their words of encouragement.

I dedicate this book to my grand children and great grandchildren to let them know how it was when I was growing up.

Special thanks to Jeri, my daughter, for her technical support on the computer.

Chapter One

Dad's Family

Dad was born and raised in a two-story log home with the customary dog trot between the main part of the house and kitchen.

Just recently I remembered my visit with Daddy's mother, Martha Angeline Holoman Myers, when I was very young, probably four or five. It was the only time I visited her without my parents.

After all these years I have a warm feeling toward Ma Myers even though I have never thought about the one time I was with her, just she and I.

That night she popped some corn over the grate using a popper made of screen wire. She let me look at things on her dresser and she had a small flat tin of pink clover leaf salve. She let me open it and smell it. I can still smell the soft fragrance of the salve and feel the smooth velvety texture on my hands. The box was white and had pictures of pink clover on the top. I would love to be able to find one of those boxes again.

Apparently I woke early the next morning since I remember she said, "You are awake?" I don't remember who I sleep with that night. Probably my grandmother since she was widow. We got up and dressed and she took me out to the kitchen which was separate from the house. As we stepped out of the house, a brown and white dog was sleeping by the step who trotted away to find some place else to sleep.

I remember she laid the kindling and started the fire. I watched the fire flare up and get going. I don't remember what she cooked for breakfast.

Later that day I was in the kitchen with Ma and Aunt Vada and I had washed my hands and when drying them on the feed sack towel which was used by everyone, I started to clean my nose with the corner of the towel and both of them yelled at me and said not to do that. Other than that I remember kindness and goodness. I feel my grandmother loved me as much as she did any of her other grandchildren.

Another time we were at Ma Myers' home and this time we went to the huge barn and picked crowder peas in a patch in front on the barn. Everyone was talking about the recent storm that went through and there was a large piece of metal roofing wrapped around a tall tree as a result of the storm.

I wish I could have spent more time with my Grandmother Myers and got to know her. Mom did not like Daddy's family and always talked unfavorably about them which led me to think they did not like me.

During the few days when my grandmother was on her death bed Dad went to their place every night and when he returned Mom would ask how she was. On the night of her death when Mom asked him how she was he replied, "Dead".

When her household items were divided we got a set of cotton grating cards and several skeins of thread that my grandmother had spun on the spinning wheel.

The cotton cards were like large wire brushes with handles and when the cotton or wool fiber was grated the cards were held one in each hand. A gob of cotton would be placed on the card and by pulling the cards the cotton would be formed into a rather large string. The sting was then put on the spinning wheel and spun into a small thread.

Mom used the cotton thread to crochet lace on some curtains for our living room. She bought some domestic (cheap unbleached muslin) and made curtains and then crocheted the lace on the edge of the curtains. They were beautiful.

We also got a walnut half bed, three of my grandmother's dresses and three cane bottom chairs. Her dresses were worn out in the seat and Mom said that was the first time she had ever seen anyone who wore out her dresses in the seat. My grandmother had a severe heart problem (heart dropsy) which explains why she sat so much and wore out her dresses in the seat.

The chairs were small and the top posts were worn down. Dad explained that he and his brothers had used them to play with as cars by pushing them around on the floor.

There was also a box of greeting cards that had never been used. They were very old and beautiful. I loved to look at them and feel the glitter on one that was a picture of a city that was lit up. The glitter was the lights. There were two or three cards with pictures of biplanes with people standing on the wings. Another card was of little chicks being pulled in a cart made of a half eggshell. They were very nice.

About the time of my grandmother's death, Dad and Mom and his brother and sisters and their spouses went to the court house in Marion, and signed the necessary forms to give their portion of the homestead to Uncle Lewis who was the oldest son.

Mom told me that when Uncle Lewis got married Dad had a job dumping tubs on top of the ground at the local mines, and he let Uncle Lewis have his job. Dad took a job under ground. It has always been hard for me to understand why the family catered to the oldest son, which is a carryover from the old country.

Dad told us one time that when he was a child he would have nightmares or bad dreams and would wake up at night crying. His parents would sit him outside on the doorstep in the dark and tell him to stay there until he could stop crying. I often wonder if my grandmother agreed to this decision. His father was supposed to have been a tyrant and I visualize Dad's mother being the kind one.

One night after we had gone to bed in the large room that we called "the house", Dad told a tale of his older brother being shot and they had to dig the bullet from his leg. I don't remember how he came to be shot. Dad said you could hear Lewis screaming for miles around.

Another time he told us that a group of hunters caught a fox and skinned it alive. After they skinned the fox it ran and got on a tree stump and howled at them. Truth or fiction I will never know.

One time he briefly touched on the bizarre behavior of the one-room school teacher who would play a game that would give her an opportunity to swing her leg high and expose her undergarments. This bizarre behavior would happen periodically and the older boys finally figured out it was during her menses.

Another time Dad told us about the time he and his brothers and some more boys from the neighborhood were swimming in a creek that ran through their property and Dad dove into the water and did not come up. One of the boys jumped into the water and dragged him out and gave him long compresses and he revived.

Every time Mom, Dennis and I would mention going swimming, Dad would tell this story and he was terrified of water. (In later years when my sons grew big and spent some time with Dad at his home, he took them swimming but not without the usual warning of the danger of the water.)

My grandfather, Isaac Myers, had two children by a previous marriage and five children by his second wife, Martha Angeline Holoman Myers. Dad was the third child.

My grandfather died when Dad was sixteen years of age and it was necessary for Dad to quit school. A strapping young boy was more valuable in the field than in the classroom.

My grandfather, Isaac Myers, was a devout Christian and taught two Sunday School classes on Sunday which isn't unusual except he taught a Baptist Class in the morning at the Crooked Creek Church and in the afternoon he taught a Methodist class at the Brown School which was in the immediate area. One of the reference books he used was "The Doctrines of Our Faith" by E.C. Dargan, D.D. who was formerly a professor of Homiletics and Ecclesiology at the Southern Baptist Theological Seminary at Louisville, KY.

My father never stepped foot in a church and I wonder if my grandfather's teachings affected him.

Dad's family led a life of deprivation and he never recovered from it. I doubt that Dad ever left Crittenden County until he visited my mother's parents in Southern Illinois.

I believe Dad found the Lord in later life because he told me one time that he liked to sit on the front porch and watch the sun go down.

Chapter 2

Grandfather Moore

The most vivid memories I have of my Grandfather Moore were his magnificent wavy hair and his beautiful singing voice. He was of Scottish descent and his hair was auburn when he was young but when I knew him his hair was gray and still had waves all around his head. I also remember the many freckles he had on his hands. Mom inherited his waves and freckles. Dennis and I inherited his wavy hair.

He would be hoeing his tomatoes and singing "Amazing Grace." Or he would be walking to town carrying a small basket of his fresh produce on his arm and singing one of his favorite hymns.

My Grandfather was a prayer warrior. He always said grace before every meal and even had prayer meetings with the family before going to bed at night. When he felt the need to pray he would do so no matter where he was or what he was doing. He liked to pray among the bushes in a field.

One of his favorite Bible verses was "If God is for you, who can be against you."

My grandfather had a knack for growing things from watermelons to potatoes. When he first retired he grew large truck patches and sold his produce. He had a small wagon and a horse which he used to haul his produce to town.

When he became too old to produce the vegetables he sold his wagon and horse to mom so she had a small wagon for going to town and doing her shopping. She only went to town one time in her little wagon and I guess because she never had any money for much shopping. Dad hitched his mule to the small wagon one time and the mule kicked the front end out of the wagon. Dad was able to repair it almost as good as new.

My Grandfather was short in stature and became stooped in his later years. My Grandmother was much taller than he in later life.

Both my Grandmothers were tall and had maternal figures.

My Grandfather was missing a forefinger of his right hand. His finger was severed in some kind of sawmill accident when he was young and the knuckle always was white.

Happiness didn't seem to be a part of my Grandfather's life. He didn't smile and always seemed on the verge of tears. He was epileptic and had to take medication and I feel that was cause for his depression.

Chapter Three

Grandmother Moore

My most vivid memory of my Grandmother Moore, Mary Elizabeth Hughes Moore, was her crocheting. She made all her dresses with large front pockets and when she would walk around the yard admiring her flowers she would carry her ball of crochet thread in her pocket and working her fingers making something beautiful. Her favorite pattern was the pineapple and she made table spreads and doilies and chair covers. Her work was always beautiful. She would give her finished product away to family members and friends.

She crocheted a pink chain collar for my grey kitten one time.

She would work in the garden in heat of the day and always wore a huge sun bonnet, which she had made, and when she came inside her face would be very red. She had beautiful fair skin and the sun never touched it. She never wore any makeup as she thought it was blasphemy. When my Grandmother passed away at age 92 the funeral director said she had the most beautiful complexion he had ever seen on an older woman.

She wore her long hair pulled back in a bun at the back of her head until she became grey when she had her hair cut and got a permanent. She no longer looked like my grandmother. That was the only time she had her hair short. She let her hair grow back out and continued to wear it in a bun.

My grandmother loved her afternoon naps. She would lie down and pull a corner of the bedspread up over her and lay her glasses on the bed beside her. Her naps drove Mom crazy. Mom would say "I don't see how anyone could pile up in bed in the middle of the day." Boy, I can and I do.

My grandmother kept water in the refrigerator in an orange colored depression-glass pitcher. It didn't have any covering on it so the water always had a peculiar taste. She had a complete set of the dishes in the early years of her marriage but along the way all the pieces except the pitcher got broken.

I remember the fresh coconut cakes my Grandmother would bake for Easter and Christmas holidays. She would buy a fresh coconut, punch a hole in the end and drain out the milk and save it for the batter of the cake. She would cut the white coconut meat out of the shell and then trim off the brown peel and grind it up. She would pile the coconut on the top and sides of the cakes. Those were the days before mixers and all the gadgets for the kitchen so she mixed her cakes by hand.

In the fall she would make pear preserves and put coconut in them which made them delicious.

My grandmother smiled a lot in spite of the fact that she was sick most of her life with ills that seemed to be imaginary however they were very real to her. When I was a little girl I remember they had a cancer scare but it turned out to be nothing.

When she was 86 years old she had a colon resection which was the most serious illness she ever had. She probably had allergies which was the cause of her respiratory problems.

When I was about ten years old my Grandmother gave us a large Bible about four inches thick. It was in large print and had lots of pictures. I read it twice that summer. A lot of it I didn't understand but I read it anyway. We had a small black Bible as the family Bible but I never saw either of my parents read it.

When the revised Bible came out she said she didn't like the new revised version and she never read the revised version. She kept her Bible handy and we would find her reading it at any moment of the day.

My grandmother also gave us a Brownie box camera but we never used since we couldn't afford film for it.

Chapter Four

Trauma in Phoenix

I n 1917 my maternal grandparents, John Wyatt Moore and Mary Elizabeth Hughes Moore went to Arizona at the suggestion of the family physician due to my grandmother's poor health with respiratory problems.

They rode the train most of the way to Arizona and used other modes of travel.

They had been in Phoenix six weeks when their beautiful 21 year old daughter, Eutha Mae, died of pneumonia. She had been engaged to a young man in Kentucky and left him behind, and went with her family. I felt that she had died of a broken heart so I wrote to the Bureau of Vital Statistics in Arizona for a copy of her death certificate and the cause of death was confirmed.

My grandmother carried guilt the rest of her life and her illnesses never got any better.

My grandfather worked in the mines and the children worked as migrant workers along with Mexicans in the cotton fields. Mom would say that their bags were weighed and that was how they were paid. The Mexicans would put rocks in their bags to make them heavier, until they got caught.

Return to Kentucky

My grandfather bought a model T car for their return trip to Kentucky. Mom liked to tell about the time they stopped on the side of the road to have a picnic and Pa drove into a pile of wet leaves and the car sank down and they had to push it out. My Grandmother was pushing and the black wet leaves splattered up onto her face and when she took off her glasses there were two white holes for her eyes. Mom would tell the story and laugh as if it was the first time she had ever told it.

In 1921 they returned to Kentucky when Mom was 14 years of age. They settled in a community known as Pilot Knob.

Dad's family lived in the area and in time my parents met.

The road was very steep up to Pilot knob and most of the road consisted of sandstone. One time Dad went to pick mom up in a buggy on a cold and icy afternoon and the horse had a hard time holding the buggy back on the ice. They used a woolen "lap robe" to keep them warm.

Mom and Dad were married September 5, 1928, and they lived with my grandparents until my grandparents moved to Southern Illinois. Mom told about the time when her grandparents were preparing to move to Illinois a neighbor said to my grandfather they would probably be lonesome when they reached Illinois. My grandfather's replay, "It will be a happy lonesome."

After my grandparents moved to Illinois, Mom and Dad continued to live in the huge white house.

Chapter Five

Life on Pilot Knob

Mom thought the house on Pilot Knob was haunted. She would hear noises in the unfinished upstairs. When she was doing something that could be done outdoors that is what she would do. She carried the churn out side under a tree or snap beans or hand sewing, anything to get out of the house.

A man had been killed at the house several years before. Some people believed that the killer had gone up the stairs and thrown the gun in the bowels of the unfinished rooms upstairs.

Many years later, my cousin, Joe King, helped tear the house down and they found the gun in the wall. Joe said the gun was so rusty it was hard to tell what kind of gun it was and the case was not reopened since all parties involved were long dead.

My Birth

When the time came for me to be born Mom went to Rosiclare, Illinois, to my Grandparent's home. They lived closer to town and the doctor. The birth was long and hard. Mom never forgot it and didn't let me forget it either. She would repeat the story of my birth often and I would always cringe and didn't know what to say. She would tell how she would beat her legs and the doctor bathed her face and brow with a cold cloth. She said if I hadn't been a very small baby we both would have died. I was breached. She carried me on a pillow due to my small size. All I can say now is that "I am sorry, sorry."

During this time in history, it was customary for an item to be placed in the hand of the newborn. It supposedly would determine what a person would become. A few hours after I was born my Grandmother put a needle, thimble and a spool of thread in my hand let me grasp it. I indeed did become a seamstress.

One of my father's sisters put money in the hand of her first born boy and he grew up to love money. So maybe there is something to the tale after all.

The Day I Ate Matches

The house on Pilot Knob was large and they only used two or three of the rooms. One day when I was around eighteen months old Mom couldn't find me.

She looked all over the place and finally found me in one of the empty rooms eating matches. She said I had eaten about three fourths of a box of the matches. As I bit off the heads of the matches, I would line them up in a little straight pile. That was when matches were made of phosphorus and I almost died. They called the doctor who induced vomiting and I only vomited up two match heads. My body swelled up three or four times the normal size. The doctor said they would have to wait for the poison to work its way out of my system. I couldn't stand for anything or anyone to touch me, not even my mother. I recovered with no noticeable side effects.

My First Memory

The first thing I remember is one day Mom and Dad were walking to see a neighbor and were carrying me in a wash tub between them. I remember their swinging the tub back and forth and telling me they were going to throw me in. When I told Mom about my first memory, she said I was about 18 months old at the time and she was surprised that I could remember at that early age.

Chapter 6

The Krauzee Place

It was some time after this that my parents moved to another farm. Dad worked at the mines at night on the swing shift and farmed during the day.

We now lived close to Mom's brother, Guthrie and his family.

The house was smaller than the one on Pilot Knob, however through my child's eyes I thought it was huge. It was an unpainted house and had boards on the sides, not siding like today, but some type of boards nailed up and down on the out side walls. It had two rooms. The great room is where we had a pot-bellied stove and our beds. It had a lean-to for a kitchen.

We had a sideboard at one end of the room and a striking clock that sat on a shelf on the wall. I remember listening for the clock to strike when I was awake during the night.

Mom kept her diamond ring in the bottom of the clock. She loved that ring and I remember seeing her put it on once in a while and holding her hand out in front of her and turning it from side to side so she could see the diamond glisten in the light. One day she went to the clock to get her ring and it wasn't there. She remarked, "I guess Lockie hocked it."

One day we found a bed of baby mice in one of the drawers of the sideboard.

They were about the size of a small thumbnail with big eyes that looked like small marbles with stretched skin over them. They were not cute like other baby animals.

I remember Mom carried them outside and tossed them in the yard.

One time Mom kept some cookies in the drawer for miscellaneous items that were shaped like someone's hands. I don't remember whose hands they were.

They were wrapped in wax paper and after many months they disintegrated into crumbs. I remember asking if I could eat them and she emphatically said "No."

The Old Cast Iron Cook Stove

In the kitchen we had a wood burning cast iron cook stove. Built into the stove, beside the firewall, was a water reservoir with a capacity of around two gallons. Our water was carried from the free-flowing spring from below the hill. Once in a while when the reservoir needed refilling Mom would tell me to carry the water up the hill and fill it. Dennis and I used empty syrup buckets for carrying the water since they were smaller than the galvanized buckets used by Mom and Dad. Even though the bucket was small whenever it was my turn to fill the reservoir I would moan. It meant I would have to make three trips up the hill before it would be full. The bail on the bucket would hurt my hands. I would be relieved when the chore was done. The hot water was appreciated by all of us.

When I married and left home and finally had indoor plumbing and all the hot water I needed, I still did not take it for granted since I would remember my small legs getting tired and the bail cutting into my hand from carrying the water up the hill when I was a little girl.

Down through the years Mom and Dad eventually were able to afford a gas cook stove and the wood burning stove was dismantled. Lord only knows what happened to the pieces of the stove and the only part this is left is the cast iron reservoir which I have today. It is painted yellow and is used as a flower pot for petunias.

The Arrival of Baby Brother

It was May 3, 1933 when I was told I was to spend the night at a neighbor's house. To this day I do not understand why I did not stay with my Aunt Augusta who lived just down the hill. Probably Aunt Augusta helped with the birthing. Anyway the lady I stayed with was elderly and had children the age of my parents.

When I returned home the next morning, Mom was in bed and told me to come to the bed and see my baby brother. I looked at him and said, "He has come to take my place." Mom became tearful and said, "Oh, Honey, no one can take your place."

I can almost recapture the feelings of abandonment as I stood there looking at my baby brother. I was about four years of age.

Dennis As A Baby

Dennis must have been a good baby since I don't remember anything about him until his second summer. Mom stated she would rather nurse him until he was through his second summer but he had several teeth and was putting them to good use. She was attempting to wean him since his teeth were getting a work out on her breast but he would not give up. He would climb upon her lap and ask to nurse and when she refused he would hit her in the chest. Of course, all these actions were very cute and amusing to my parents. Mom became more and more determined to wean him and put many things on her nipples to discourage him. She used iodine and even soot but he would nurse as if he could taste nothing. He would raise his head and smile at me after nursing and around his mouth would be black with soot.

During the weaning process Dennis became very ill. One night at the time Dad was leaving for work, Dennis woke up with a high temperature, vomiting and diarrhea. Dad was working the "graveyard" shift so it was about 10:30 pm. Mom told me to run after Dad and have him come back. I ran out of the house into the night and down the path that was unfamiliar at night. I had never been away from the house alone at night and I remember being afraid but ran on and started calling Dad. In a few minutes I caught up to him and told him about the problem and he said he had better go back even though he didn't want to miss work.

Dennis had the "summer complaint" which happened in the second year of a child's life. We almost lost him that summer. He became dehydrated and that was when he decided he didn't need the breast anymore. Mom was very worried and one day she said, "I have tried everything I know to try." She seemed resigned to that fact she cold not save him. I don't remember anything being said about getting a doctor but seems as if someone did say that there wasn't anything a doctor could do.

One day a strange man was walking through the community and learned about Dennis' illness. He told mom he could save the baby. He gave her explicit instructions about how to dress a young chicken, leave it whole, cram it into a glass jar, not put any water in the jar with the chicken, and put a tight lid on the jar, and put the jar into a pan of water and cook until the chicken was done. He told her to then spoon feed the broth from the chicken to Dennis. Mom did this and I remember our waiting patiently the several hours it took for the chicken to cook. As soon as the chicken was done she began feeding Dennis a spoon full of the broth at a time. In a few hours he began eating and drinking and in a few days he was back to normal.

I like to think the strange man was an angel.

Potty Training

Another traumatic experience was the potty training. Each time Dennis needed to "go" he wanted to pull all his clothes off. We had "outside" toilet facilities. One day Dennis needed to "go" and had promptly stripped and was running around the yard when one of our neighbor women came up the road. There was a good deal of yelling from Mom at him to get dressed. My memory fails me as to how Mom finally accomplished the toilet training.

Some time after Dennis recovered from the summer complaint Mom made him two summer suits from seersucker fabric that was green and white and tan and white. When she finished the little green one she dressed Dennis in his new suit complete with shoes and socks. We then walked to the field where Dad was plowing so Dad could see Dennis all dressed up. I remember how cute Dennis was walking along in front of us with his little back so straight like small children do.

When we got to where Dad was working he and Mom admired Dennis in his fine clothes.

Chapter Seven

Dennis' Antics

When Dennis was quite small, around two or three years old, he would wave his spoon around at the dinner table, and threaten to throw it. He would say, "Here it come, here it comes," and would finally throw it. Mom and Dad thought this was so cute and laughed at him. I don't remember how they broke him of this awful habit.

One time Dennis kept acting up and Mom had to correct him several times.

Finally she sat him down in a chair and said, "You had better toe the mark." Dennis sat there for a few minutes and then said, "I am toeing it." Mom said, "What?" "I am toeing the mark." Dennis replied. There he sat with both big toes pointed at a black pattern in the linoleum covering on the floor.

Dennis would always run from Mom when she attempted to spank him. One day he ran up a tree and wouldn't come down. Finally after much coaxing he came down and fell spraining his ankle. Mom thought it was broken and the doctor was called but it was just a sprain.

One summer there was a huge yellow jackets nest in one of our peach trees. Dennis was fascinated by the nest and started throwing rocks at it. Mom told him not to throw rocks at the nest because he was going to get stung. So then he climbed up into the tree with a broom handle and proceeded to poke at the nest. The yellow jackets came swarming out and stung him in many places. Mom put soda plasters on the stings. Needless to say he stayed clear of the nest after that.

When Dennis and I were still young Mom had Dad buy some sand and he dumped it in a hole near the side of the yard. Dennis and I spent many hours in the sand pile. One day as I sat in the sand playing Dennis threw a half brick and hit me on the head. It made a gash and blood spewed everywhere. I never figured out why Dennis hit me. I have a theory, though. Mom was onto me all the time so he thought I was their common enemy and he hit me.

The first word that Dennis said is not remembered but most likely it was a swear word. Dad was a tremendous curser and when Dennis started to imitate him, Mom and Dad would laugh and remark how cute it was and at the same time they would wonder how they could prevent his learning more of the same.

As Dennis grew older, all the animals around the farm got a dose of his torrential swearing. When he attempted to train a goat to pull his cart the goat was having difficulty getting the hang of what he was supposed to do and Dennis would shower him with his usual swearing and would bite the goat's ears to drive the point home. The goat would shake his head and jump around but finally settled down. The goat did learn to pull the cart but he was inconsistent with his submissiveness and often would take off in a run with the cart twisting and flying behind him. The goat finally tore the cart all to pieces.

Dennis decided he would teach our old bulldog "Black" to pull a cart. He took a dynamite box and mounted it on two wheels is about all I can remember about the construction of the cart, but I do remember how faithful the boxy-built black dog would pull two gallons of water up the hill from the spring. He would not take his time to keep from getting tired out but wanted to run. He would get so tired he would practically collapse. His tongue would be hanging out with saliva dripping.

Dennis had a way with animals. He taught a calf to let us ride him. At a matter of fact we rode two calves. When the calf would be in his stall eating, we would climb up the boards which made the stall and onto his back and sit there while he was eating. Pretty soon we could ride him when he was loose. We would ride the calf just about everywhere around the farm and down to see our Aunt Vada. I don't remember why we stopped riding the first calf, probably because it got too large. Many times our cousin, Harold Glenn, would join us but then we decided all three of us were too heavy for the calf so one of us would walk while two rode. We took turns riding and walking.

Language came easy for Dennis and he liked to sing and make up cute sayings. We had a neighbor whose name was "Jim." Dennis made up a little song about him. "Dinky, donkey, Jim, had a wife who couldn't swim." He would sing it to our neighbor much to the delight to the two of them. After that Dennis was forever called "Dinky."

Chapter Eight

Clothing

When Dennis and I were pre-school age Mom made most of our clothes. We hardly got anything new unless Mom made it. She would make my dresses and I never had many clothes at one time. I remember wearing my food caked dresses for two or three days and since I dribbled my food the dresses were always coated with soup drips. I don't know how old I was before I finally got the hang of how to eat without dribbling.

One summer the owner of the farm that we were share cropping came by to visit us. She was older than Mom but had a small boy. As usual my dress was stiff in front and Mom was extremely embarrassed and kept apologizing to Mrs. Krauzee about my untidy appearance.

A short time after that a box of clothes came for me. There were several little dresses that were smocked, embroidered, and tucked with white collars and cuffs.

Mom was so excited about the beautiful clothes that the first chance she got she dressed me up in one of the dresses and rolled my air on rags and caught a ride to town with

Uncle Guthrie and had our pictures made. Dennis was about three years old and it was the first picture we had of him. Mom really regretted not having a picture of him when he was a baby. Dennis and I had to ride in the rumble seat of Uncle Guthrie's car and we got caught in a rain and got wet. We had the picture made anyway.

Also in the package with the clothes was a big doll with real eye lashes and real human hair. Mrs. Krauzee said they had named the doll "Marie Antoinette." She sent several dresses for the doll, a coat with fur collar, shoes and a little bed. The bed was wooden and large enough for the doll to sleep on. The doll, clothes and bed gave me many hours of pleasure.

The time Mrs. Krauzee came to see us was in enquiry my Dad made with the banker who was the contact person for the property. Someone was cutting timber along the fence row and Dad thought it might be on the Krauzee property. The banker contacted the Krauzee family in St. Louis and she came to inspect the timber cutting. Mom told me to go with her and show her where the cutting was taking place. While I waited in the car for her to go look at the property she left her little boy in the car with me. While she was out of the car the little boy swung on the steering wheel of the car and I wondered if he was going to tear up the car. When Mrs. Krauzee saw what he was doing she told him to stop it.

Someone gave me a red chinchilla coat with matching hat and I felt like a little princess in it. We had been somewhere for the night and caught a ride with someone coming to another mines that was within walking distance to our house. It was still dark and while we were walking home I noticed that I didn't recognize my red coat in the dark. It had become a dark unidentifiable color.

When it came time for me to start to school Mom asked Uncle Guthrie to get enough fabric for two dresses for me. (Uncle Guthrie had a car and went to town more often than we did.) He got some red and white checked fabric and the other was yellow and white. Mom devised her own simple pattern and it was magical how the dresses materialized. I thought Mom was a genius.

One time Mom used walnut hulls to make a dye. She dyed a piece of unbleached muslin a nice brown and made herself a dress. The dress was an a-line affair. She only dyed cloth that one time. Probably the fabric faded is why she didn't do it again.

Mom made herself two dust caps. They were pointed affairs and she wore them when cleaning the house, or sweeping down cobwebs. She wore them until they got soiled and never washed them and ironed them for use a second time. I guess she decided they were too much trouble.

One winter I needed a coat and Mom went to a second-hand store. She took me with her and we tried on one or two but she decided on a tan boys' overcoat with buttons on the wrong side. She said that it was a boys' coat but since it was wool and very warm she decided to buy that one. I enjoyed the warmth but always wished the buttons and holes cold be switched. Even Mom's sewing expertise could not remedy that problem.

Aunt Augusta would give me Harold's cast-off overalls since he was about two years older than me. By the time he outgrew them they were just right for wearing. They were soft and comfortable. If they needed mending I would patch them and couldn't wait to put them on. I could climb trees and not get my legs scratched.

I wore long stockings to school in the winter time. They were held up with a homemade garter. One day after school

I told my Mom that my stocking had a run and asked if she would repair it for me to wear to school the next day. She was busy and couldn't get to it so I got a thimble, thread and needle and repaired it myself. I took tiny stitches and when mom saw it she was surprised at my mending ability.

Mending is still a pleasure to me since I love to make things whole again.

One time someone gave Mom some cast-off shoes. There was a pair of tennis shoes that were worn out and Mom had to regrettably throw them away. I remember her stating that she sure wished they were good enough to wear since she knew they would be comfortable. Another pair was with heels and she was unable to work around the farm wearing them. She took the shoes to the wood pile, used the axe to cut the heels down a comfortable height. When she put them on the toes pointed straight up. It was a funny sight.

On another occasion Mrs. Krauzee sent us a box of clothing that contained two dresses for Mom. They were satin and crepe material and dressier than what Mom could use. She did use one for a pattern and made herself one from cotton material. She made pointed cuffs and when she got it finished and wore it around the house, but she decided the pointed cuffs got in her way doing dishes so she cut the cuffs off.

We received the customary catalogs through the mail, such as Sears and Montgomery Ward.

It was so much fun looking at all the beautiful things in them and dream about the things we could never have. One time I saw a pinafore in the catalog that I dearly loved so I asked Mom to make me one. She said she would have to wait until she went to town to get the fabric for it. I got impatient for her to make it so she cut up an old pillow slip and made the pinafore out of that. I loved it.

Chapter Nine

Our Water Supply

There was a free-flowing fresh-water spring on our farm which supplied our household water, everything from cooking to bathing. Mom would clean out the spring every few months and it was like a miracle to see the clear cold water bubbling out of the ground.

The spring water must have had a good supply of minerals since Dennis and I had no cavities until we were adults.

In later years when we had moved to Illinois the mines in the community were flooded and the spring dried up never to flow again.

The spring flowed into a creek that was a few feet from the spring. The creek water was used for laundry at times. Not far above the spring area was a deeper hole in the creek where water would stand after the creek had stopped flowing due to lack of rain. One summer Harold, Dennis and I were playing around the hole and saw a huge bullfrog jump into the hole. We decided he had some luscious legs so we decided to bail out the water hole and get the frog so we could have some frog legs. We went to the house and gathered up syrup buckets and each of us had one. After many hours of dipping and pouring we spotted the frog hugging the bottom of the hole. We scooped him up and Harold promptly slaughtered him and cut off his legs. We ran to the house and had Mom get us a skillet and some grease and we proceeded to fry the frog legs. Lo and behold, when the legs got hot they started to jump and it looked as if they were going to jump right out of the skillet. It was as if they were still alive. I didn't have much stomach for the legs after that but since I had never tasted frog legs I gave it a try and found that they were extremely good.

Chapter Ten

The Bay Lady

One Day when I was around five years old I heard a horse coming up the road by our house. I ran to the end of our yard and looked out over the washed out road bed.

As I stood there watching her guide the beautiful bay mare even my inexperienced eyes recognized the respect between horsewoman and horse. She carried her like a Dresden doll. When she came even with me she said, "Hi, Honey." I replied, "Hi." The woman was so elegant it made me conscious of my soiled dress.

I watched the lady ride on down the road and wondered who she was.

I ran into the house and told Mom about her but Mom wasn't very impressed. For several days thereafter I would think of the woman on the horse and vowed that when I grew up I would be just like her.

Chapter Eleven

Wash Day

One spring day when the weather was warm and inviting, Mom decided to haul her laundry down to the spring, rather than carry the water up the hill to the house. Even with the help of "Old Black" it was always a chore. Mom liked to use lots of water and she said that was the secret of nice clean clothes. So this summer we set up the iron kettle by the side of the creek which ran along the spring. The water for the laundry was taken from the creek and we used the fresh spring water for our personal use. Mom strung her clothes line between two trees and we spent the whole day down by the spring. For our "dinner" she baked sweet potatoes in the ashes in the fire under the kettle.

One wash day I was playing with a rusty tin can and was trying to dip some water from the kettle for something, I can't remember what for, and since the water was too hot I just left the tin can in the kettle. When Mom saw the rusty tin can in her hot wash water she started yelling and got a stick, lifted the tin can out of the hot water and slung it right onto my ankle. I started screaming and ran and got into the creek and stood there in the cool water and watched my skin fold down over my sock top. Of course mom was very sorry about the whole thing and was very good with her home remedies and gave me lots of attention during the healing process. I remember I got a limb which I used for a make-shift crutch. I liked the extra attention Mom was giving me and I asked for a bought crutch, but Mom set me straight right quick by telling me that I didn't need a crutch.

One day I was standing beside the wash tub where Mom was scrubbing a pair of Dad's soiled overalls. I asked her, "Mom, I wonder who that woman was." She asked, "Who?" I said, "You know, the lady on the bay horse who rode by the house other day." Mom replied, "I don't know. It might have been your imagination again. If she was as pretty and nicety as you said, I bet she never has to wash any overalls. She just rides around on that horse all day." Mom said as she twisted the stubborn fabric overalls to get the water out of them.

Chapter Twelve

Food Preparation and Preservation

Our meals were basic southern cooking with biscuits and cornbread as well. When we had company Mom would fix both breads. She had a cast iron cornbread stick pan which she used for baking her cornbread. It was always crunchy and so good. (I still have the pan.)

I remember opening a hot fresh homemade biscuit, popping fresh churned butter on it with a gob of home canned blackberry jam and no one standing in the background yelling fat and sugar.

White beans and potatoes were served almost every day.

During the summer when the gardens were producing and in the winter time when we slaughtered hogs we had lots of food.

The gardens were huge and produced everything from lettuce and radishes in the spring to cashew pumpkins, turnips and greens in the fall. I remember the huge heads of cabbage and the many bowls of coleslaw made with the cabbage and remember the large crockery jar she would make kraut in. She would shred the cabbage and add salt to it to make the kraut. She would put a piece of wood on the top of the jar but when the kraut pushed the wood off, she put a large rock on it to hold it down. She would pour off the brine every day or so and when there was no brine the kraut was done.

At hog killing time Mom would make sausage with lots of sage and cram it into a cloth sack she made from domestic. (cheap unbleached muslin) We would cure the meat with some kind of curing compound purchased at the store.

In June or July Mom would pick many buckets of blackberries and can them. She would boil the jars in a large tub, along with the lids and rubber rings so they were germ free. She also canned tomatoes, green beans, and corn. She had trouble getting the corn to not spoil, though. The tomatoes were used for homemade soup in the winter.

One summer Mom dried some apples. She put me upon the house with some sheets and had me spread the apples on the sheets to dry. While I was up there a plane flew over and I waved at it. Someone in the plane put something white up to the window. I said no one saw me but Mom said, "Yes, they did. Didn't you see the white paper at the window?"

We tackled cider making one fall and then another time Uncle Guthrie made molasses on his farm. I don't remember much about the cider making but the molasses making is a vivid memory. There was a large flat pan where the juice from the cane was boiled and I remember sucking on the crushed cane and cutting my lips. There was a mule that went round and round to run the cane through press to force out the juice. It was so much fun watching the juice boil.

In the spring time when the squash was in full bloom, Mom would walk along the rows and examine the blooms and when she recognized blooms that were not going to produce a squash she would pull those blooms. She would take them to the house, wash them and roll them in a flour and egg batter and fry them. That was a delicacy that we really enjoyed. When she removed the unproductive blooms this enhanced the growth of the other blooms.

I wish I had asked Mom to show me how to recognize the unproductive blooms, but never did. Maybe some day I will run across someone who can recognize the unproductive blooms of squash and teach me how it is done.

One spring day Mom picked some fresh corn and fried it for our lunch. She sat the bowl on the table and Dennis and I ate the entire bowl of new fried corn. Mom said, "You kids ate all the corn and now I will have to fix something else for your Daddy.

Dad built a barn close to the house for storing the feed and milking the cows.

Most of the time during the winter months, Dad would have to buy commercial feed for the animals. It was very expensive so he wouldn't buy it if it wasn't absolutely necessary.

One morning we didn't have anything for breakfast so Mom gave me a pan and told me to go out to the barn and get some bran that was in a sack for the cows. I got the bran and took it back to the kitchen and Mom mixed it with water and boiled it for us for our breakfast. We had biscuits with it. I remember how good it was and very wholesome food.

I don't remember how many times we had the bran for breakfast, but it was probably until the next trip to town.

These are two examples of how Mom was sporadic with her meal planning. I don't now if we were really out of food or if Mom was in one of her periods of depression and could not think it through as to how to prepare a meal. I remember she would be very glum and never smiled.

One summer blackbirds kept swarming around our house and in the trees. They were a real nuisance. They were there for several days and Mom kept fussing about the noise.

One day she took the shot gun and shot into the swarm of birds. They really scattered and dead birds fell from the sky. Mom gathered up all the dead birds and cleaned them and made them into a pie. I remember she counted eighteen birds. She made the crust and put the skinned and gutted birds in the crust and then baked the pie. The birds were so tough we couldn't eat the pie so she threw it out.

The shot gun had such a powerful recoil that she complained of her shoulder hurting for several days from the "kick" from the gun.

That was the only time she tried making a blackbird pie.

One time when we were on our way to visit my Grandmother Myers in the wagon, Mom spotted some horehound growing along the road. She had Daddy stop the wagon so she got out and pulled some of the horehound up. We took the horehound home and she made some fresh horehound candy. She pulled it like taffy and it was delicious.

Chapter Thirteen

School

First Grade

There were two or three one-room schools in the community where we lived. Mom and Dad started me at one that was on the way to town known as "Bethel."

A cousin, Harold Glenn Moore, who was one or two years older than me, walked with me.

I don't remember much about my first grade except a bigger boy told me one time that a calf was following me. When I told him I didn't know what he was talking about he said, "The calf muscle in your leg."

One beautiful sunny day several of us girls were sitting out under a tree eating our lunches and I was unable to get my jelly pail open. I tried and tried and then I began hitting it. About that time I saw Mom and Dennis walking up to the school. She got the lid off for me and told me not to hit it any more. I guess I was frustrated. They went on their way to her friends' house. That was the only time she put my lunch in the jelly pail. She called her friend "Mrs. Red".

In the fall, our teacher took us on a hike through the woods. We gathered colored leaves and picked some wild grapes that were growing on vines in the woods.

Our reader was "Little Black Sambo". It was my introduction to black people. When the yellow tigers circled and circled until they turned to butter didn't make much of an impression on me since I knew that wasn't how you made butter. I had helped my mother churn butter enough to know that was a falsehood.

One day our first-grade teacher read us a poem about 20 froggies as follows:

Twenty froggies went to school
Down by a rushing pool
Twenty coats all pressed and green
Twenty vests all white and clean.

We must be in time said they;
First we study then we play
That is how we learn the rules
As we froggies go to school.
Master bullfrog brave and stern
Taught us how to leap and dive
Also how to nobly stride;
Taught us how to dodge below
From the sticks which bad boys throw.
Twenty froggies grew up fast
Big frogs they became at last,
Polished to a high degree
As each froggy ought to be.
Now they sit on other logs
Teaching other little frogs.

I remember my crayons and loved the vivid colors. It was like magic how you could rub the crayon on the paper and make colorful pictures.

I remember how I would erase many times and rub holes in my rough paper that was used for beginners. I asked Daddy to get some smooth paper that I could erase and not make holes.

Sometime during the later part of the school year a bastard boy beat me up. I don't know why, since I had no contact with him prior to the beating.

We had to pass by the house where the boy lived with several other children. A large boy in the eighth grade walked us down the road almost to my house making sure I was all right.

While we were walking along, we saw a praying mantis perched on a weed and the bigger boy told me and Harold that the praying mantis could spit poison many feet and put out our eyes.

The next fall Mom enrolled me in another one-room school that was south of our house called "Siloam." I went there until the seventh grade when we moved to Southern Illinois

Second to Seventh Grades

I had to walk to school alone when I changed schools. There was an old road bed that I walked and across the fields of our neighbors. I was not afraid until I saw snakes.

Since I walked across a field it was necessary for me to climb over two fences. It seems there was a stile at one of the fences.

On winter mornings, the Jack Frost was beautiful pushing up out of the ground. I liked to eat it. It was crunchy and would break off up and down and not straight across. It was smooth like whipped ice.

Walking during the winter was really nicer since there wasn't anything crawling.

At a very early age, I learned to read and loved books. The first books I was introduced to were my father's school books which I loved. I remember one about the American Indian which I liked most of all.

One day I told Mom about envisioning a covered bridge across the path that I walked to school. The covered bridge would protect me from the rain, sleet and hail and also the snakes.

Another day I saw several kids walking down the road toward their homes and I thought, "I wish I had someone to walk with." So the next day I went with them. We walked quite a distance and one by one all of them got to their homes and I was alone. I continued on the road to my house and it was a long walk. The road was new to me. The only thing I knew about the road was that our mailman drove over it every day. I trudged along and finally got home. Mom was worried about me since I was extremely late. I told her the reason I went the long route and she told me not to go that way again. She didn't have to tell me that because I knew from my tired legs that I wouldn't attempt it again.

Foreign Behavior

For a few months a neighbor girl walked part of the way with me. We would meet at a corner of a field. She came from one angle and I another and we would cross the fence and walk on to school together. She was an older girl and towered over me.

Not only was she much taller than I was but she was chubby. We didn't get along very well and I remember we argued most of the time. One afternoon we were saying "so long" at our parting place and I let go of a mouth full of spit and spat it right on her broad freckled face. I still remember the startled look on her face. As I stood there watching my spit trickle down her face, she asked very calmly, "Jewell , why did you do that?" It was impossible for me to answer. I did not know why I did it, and I was as stunned as she was. Neither did I say I was sorry. Maybe it was because I wasn't. I don't remember seeing her any more after that.

The farmer whose field I walked through had a cow die and the carcass lay close to where I would walk. The buzzards were numerous and would feed on the carcass and then fly up into a tree nearby and puke. Until the carcass was completely gone I walked a wide girth around it.

If I walked the road and not across the field, the distance was a great deal farther. There was an abandoned house on the road and I would peep through the window and could see all the furniture still in it just as if it was waiting for their owner to come home. There was an old treadle sewing machine sitting by a window, which made it easy to see.

Since I walked alone to school, Mom started my brother, Dennis, to school when he was five years old. Dennis never liked school and mom thought it was because she started him at an early age. The fall that Dennis started to school, the teacher had Dennis and me to sit together due to lack of seats.

I would color pictures in Dennis' first grade book and the teacher told me not to do it again. One of the things I colored was a dog bowl and I put polka dots on it. When I did it a second time she said if I didn't stop coloring in Dennis book she would have to contact my parents, so I never did it again. I could never figure out how she knew it was me doing the coloring.

I would read the books that our teacher checked out at the local library. One time I turned in a book and asked the teacher for another one but she said I had read all the books she had so I would have to wait until she got some more. One of the books I tried to read was "Alice in Wonderland" which I didn't like. It was too frivolous for my pragmatic mind.

Our teacher gave us a Bible for learning verses. I remember trying very hard to memorize the verses. When we had remembered the number of assigned verses, we were given a nice small Bible.

When I was in the fourth grade Mom taught me the little poem called "Are You Sleeping?" I sang it in school much to the teacher's delight. It is as follows:

> Fre're Jacques, Fre're Jacques,
> Dormez-vous. Dormez-vous?
> Sonnez les matines,
> Sonnez les matines,
> Din, din, don. Din, Din, don
> Are you sleeping, Are you sleeping
> Brother John, Brother John?
> Morning bells are ringing,
> Morning bells are ringing,
> Ding, ding, dong. Ding, ding, dong.

Halloween

One Halloween night some pranksters put feces in a water cup and put it into our desk. The stench was terrible. We didn't tell anyone about it and left it there until one day every one was outside at the opposite side of the school building so I rushed in and grabbed the cup of feces and slung it out the back door. I made sure no one else was around, so no one saw me.

Another Halloween I made a costume out of an old white pillow slip. The two corners were pulled up and tied with string for ears and I cut holes for the face. The teacher gave me first prize.

Christmas Gift for Teacher

One Christmas Mom bought some writing pens for gifts. She bought some yellow ones and some black ones. She took the tops off the yellow ones and put them on the black ones which made each pen two colors. The teacher said he liked them better that way.

Friends

Since I was very shy I didn't make friends readily.

One Christmas one of my girl friends asked me if I would like to exchange gifts and I said yes. I don't remember what I got for her, but she got me a handkerchief with Maureen O'Hara on it. Another Christmas a girl gave me a manicure kit.

One time I invited a girl to spend the night with me. We slept together. She had to get up during the night so I told her to get a peach from the basket sitting in the kitchen. She came back to bed and ate the peach and tossed the seed out the window, except there was a screen on the window and the seed fell to the floor.

One sunny day some of us girls were sitting on the front porch of the school and a girl asked me to comb her hair. I took the comb and began combing her hair and then I noticed the yellow dandruff piled up on her scalp and my stomach turned over. Our teacher was standing there watching us and she noticed my reaction. Immediately I stopped combing and the girl said, "Keep on combing", but I dropped the comb and ran out into the school yard.

For some reason one of the older girls latched onto me and asked me to go places and do things with her during lunch break. We visited a black family who lived close to our school, and they had a new baby so we visited them and told them we had come to see the new baby. There were several adults sitting on the front porch. We were there for a while when the mother said the baby needed to be changed. She came back out on the porch with the baby and we left shortly after. I regretted not being able to see the baby's bottom. That afternoon when I got home I told Mom about going to visit the black family and she bawled me out good. "Don't you ever go back about those people."

So we didn't.

Another day the girl and I went for a walk during lunch and she suggested we go skinny dipping in a waterhole in a creek across the road from the school. The hole was in some bushes and no one could see us. I took off my clothes and sank into the cool water that took my breath away. I didn't like the water on my body. I don't remember the girl undressing. She just sat on the bank and watched me splash around.

Another time, or it might have been the time we went skinny dipping, the girl suggested that we take some apples from a tree that grew nearby. We gathered up a bunch of apples and put them in our skirts and went back to school. School had already taken up when we got back and the teacher really gave us a tongue lashing about stealing the apples. That episode ended my friendship with the older girl since I decided I didn't want to get into any more trouble.

Pie Auction

One time our teacher had a pie auction so Mom made a raisin pie and marked the package some how so Dad could know which one was Mom's so he could bid on it. So that is what they did and they came home with the pie that they had taken to the school. I never knew why Mom didn't want anyone else to buy her pie.

Wasp Sting

One day during class, I asked permission to go to the outhouse and when I opened the door of the outhouse, a wasp stung me on my shoulder through my dress. It hurt like the devil. Later in the day a boy who had been looking out the window, asked me if I got stung and I told him that it had. But there had been no tears.

Ghosts

One day when we were all outside playing in the school yard, I happened to look across the field up on a hill at the cemetery. The tombstones were changing places as if they were playing tag. I watched them for several minutes and I looked and saw some of the other kids were watching as well. I don't know why we didn't say anything about what we saw.

Teachers

Usually our teacher was a woman but about every other year we would get an elderly man by the name of Mr. Foster for a teacher. He was never in a good mood and yelled at the students a lot. I do remember he always started the school day with our singing a few hymns. I liked that. Also I remember our singing Christmas songs for a Christmas Program.

Reading Problems

It must have been when I was about in fourth grade when we were having reading class one day. One of the students was older and very tall, maybe about 14 or so. When the teacher asked him to read, he stood slumped, held his book in his left hand and clasped his right hand on his left wrist. The teacher had to tell him almost every other word. It was very painful watching him struggle with the words. The teacher looked at him quizzically, and after what seemed a very long time, she told him to take his seat.

Move to Illinois

The day we moved to Illinois, I rode in the cab of the truck, and when we passed the school I looked out the window and saw the children playing in the school yard. A lump came up in my throat and Mr. Fritts, the man who was driving, made some kind of remark about my missing the school.

I fought back tears.

School Transformed

Several years ago when we passed the school going to visit my parents in Southern Illinois, we noticed that the school had been made into a residence and was attractive with the lawn landscaped with flowers growing everywhere. The building was painted yellow with green shutters.

I would like to stop and ask the residents if they got stung by wasps when they tore down the old out house and if they ever stand out in the front yard and watch the tombstones at the cemetery on the distant hill play tag.

*Mary Eula, Eutha Mae, Tommy, Guthrie, Mary
Elizabeth Hughes Moore, and John Wyatt Moore*

Home in Phoenix where the Moore Family
lived when Eutha Mae died

Eutha Mae Moore died 1917

John Lockie and Mary Eula Moore Myers

Jewell Evelyn Myers and Dennis Ray
Myers made around 1933

William Isaac Myers

Martha Angeline Holloman Myers

John Wyatt and Mary Elizabeth Hughes Moore

Jessie and Mary Belle Fritz Myers with son, Robert

Guthrie and Augusta Hughes Moore

Harold Glenn Moore

Chapter Fourteen

Mom's Home Remedies

M om had a great respect for the nursing profession. She spoke with pride about her older sister having been a nurse. Mom was very adept at treating whatever ailed us from burns to nail punctures.

We lived as tenant farmers in Crittenden county, KY. The nearest doctor was several miles away in Marion, KY. We had no phone so when we had an injury or serious illness, getting a message to the doctor took considerable coordination. Dad would track down a neighbor who was going to town and ask him to give the doctor a message that he was needed on the Krauzee Farm by the Myers Family. The doctor wasn't called unless the illness was serious or if there were an injury. (None of us ever had any broken bones, however, we had some severe strains.)

My grandparents had relocated to Arizona when Mom was about 9 years old. She must have spent a great deal of time with the Native Americans since she knew many remedies practiced by the Indians. Mom could identify every tree in the forest and would indicate if it had any medicinal properties.

My memories of Mom are more vivid during times of illness. She would always come forth with lots of attention and because of comments she made I realized she felt that she had neglected me. She would over-do her nursing to compensate for her imagined neglect. Consequently I came to kind of like being sick since the extra attention was comforting.

Mom would cut the bark from a sycamore tree and boil it in water making a tea. The tea was used for applying to any type of rash to stop the itching. When my brother, Dennis, and I contracted poison ivy she had us drink the fresh sycamore tea and she put a cup of the fluid in our bath water and we never got poison ivy or poison oak again.

She used the inner bark of the slippery elm tree boiled in water for making waving solution for our hair. Our hair waved naturally and the solution enhanced the curl.

Bruised peach tree leaves tied up in a white cloth were used in the rinse water for whitening the wash. The chlorophyll in the leaves acted the same way as the whitening agent "bluing", which most of the farm wives used in those days because bleach was not on the market yet.

In the springtime we were treated to the customary sassafras tea. We would take a shovel into the woods and search for a tree that grew its roots close to the surface of the ground and dig the roots out. There were two kinds of sassafras so we would have to search until we found a red one. We would take the fresh roots to the house, wash them, and peel the soft bark from the root and then boil it in water.

The tea was refreshing. It was used to thin the blood in the springtime. I would like to know if it would lower cholesterol in the blood.

Also in the springtime we would gather greens such as poke, and both wide and narrow docks. A tea made from the wide dock would reduce swelling from a strained muscle such as sprained ankle. The greens were used as a substitute for turnip greens or spinach.

One summer Dennis and I had almost recovered from the Chicken Pox, and after Mom had done her laundry in the back yard by the house and she gave us a bath in the rinse water since it was still clear. Apparently I wasn't completely over the Chicken Pox because I developed pneumonia. I remember being very ill and in bed, but it wasn't until I started spitting up blood that a doctor was called.

"Old Doc Frazier" from Marion came from town in his buggy or horseback and took out his thermometer and stuck it under my arm. I was always afraid of the little glass thing and eyed his black bag with apprehension. He told Mom I had pneumonia and gave her two large white pills with the instruction to dissolve them each in a cup of water and give me a spoonful of the solutions every four hours. In a few days I had fully recovered.

Another time I had an ache in my stomach and side. Mom finally had Dr. Frazier come see me and he said he did not know what was wrong since I was very young (six or seven) to have the symptoms. He prescribed mineral oil which I took for several weeks and the oil would run out on my panties and soil them. The soiled panties were an inconvenience so I discontinued the mineral oil after a few weeks. When I became an adult and was diagnosed as having a spastic colon then I realized the problem I had as a child was the start of that problem.

One time I had dizziness and Mom was trying to determine what was causing it. My Grandmother Moore came to see us and noticed that I was spending a lot of time swinging. One morning I got up and when I looked out the back door, I noticed that my swing was tied up so high I couldn't get to it. I stated protesting and my grandmother told me she thought if I didn't swing for a few days my dizziness would go away. She must have been right, since I don't remember being dizzy after that and neither do I remember ever swinging again.

Dennis and I had the customary earaches and Mom would warm "sweet" oil and put a drop in each ear. If the pain were severe, Dad would blow smoke in the ear. That was the only time I ever saw dad smoke and I don't know what he smoked since there were never any cigarettes around the house. He probably smoked grapevine since is what comes to mind or possibly "rabbit tobacco".

We had the usual childhood injuries around the farm such as stepping on rusty nails, stubbed toes, bee stings, bruises and sore feet from walking barefoot on stones and stubbles. It was probably the summer between my first year and second year in school that Mom told me to go barefooted during the summer to save my shoes for school in the fall. I went barefooted for several days and one day I told Mom about my feet being sore from walking on the stubs where the weeds had been mowed.

She looked at my feet and said, "Your feet are a mess. You had better wear your shoes after all." I gladly put on my shoes and never tried to go barefoot again.

For the nail punctures Mom would soak our foot in hot water and then put it in a large pail with a smoking woolen cloth. The smoke was produced from a woolen cloth lighted just enough to smoke but no flames. She would wrap a towel around the top of the pail to keep the smoke from escaping from the pail. We always healed and did not have any ill effects.

Bee stings were treated with soda pack made with small amount of water and soda.

I remember the head colds and Vicks salve, the mustard plasters or onion plasters and the warm "outing" flannel cloth on our chests and around our necks. On the whole all of us were healthy and only had the usual bumps and scrapes. Dennis and I didn't have the measles until we moved to Illinois when we were much older.

One summer my legs ached for weeks. Even during the day I would have to go to bed and get them warm. Mom put Dennis' white iron crib out under a tree so I could sleep in it during the day where it was cooler. Mom was afraid I was taking a strange sounding disease called "Polio." Eventually the pain stopped and I returned to normal. To this day I do not know why I had the pain in my legs.

One summer Mom decided she needed a cellar under the house. She sharpened the hoe to where the steel blade was bright and went to work. Mom was a strong woman and she had dug a sizeable hole when she had to break and prepare lunch for all of us. She didn't get back to her project for a day or so and I started playing in the hole. The freshly dug earth was a cool place on the hot summer days. About the second time I played in the hole I slipped and my foot hit the sharp hoe and almost severed my right big toe. Mom bandaged the cut closed and treated it with a brown ointment which they referred to as "carbolic salve" and it healed nicely with stiffness the only after effect.

A separate can of the "carbolic salve" was kept at the barn for treating the animals for cuts and insect bites. Our cows had lumps on their backs where some insect laid it's larvae and a lump would grow underneath the skin. These growths were referred to as "wolves." Mom would pry the larvae out and put the "carbolic salve" on the wounds so they would heal.

I don't remember Mom and Dad being sick except for one time Mom had a "crick" in her neck and Dad had

Malaria symptoms. Mom would buy bulk quinine and empty capsules and fill the capsules with the quinine to give to Dad for aches and chills due to the Malaria. She gave me quinine for a cold and it made my ears ring.

Another time I remember Mom bought some loose sulfur and gave it to Dennis and me in a spoon with molasses. I don't know what that was for, but I liked the sulfur taste.

One day Mom sent me to school with a wad of asphidia tied up in a rag attached to a string around my neck. It was to "keep off germs." When I told her about the kids questioning me about it at school she never made me wear it again. It was tossed off as being superstition anyway. It indeed did keep off the germs, all friends, relatives, pets and insects. The smell was terrible.

Mom loved to read about illnesses and how to cure them. One time she sent off for a book complete with colored pictures. I remember the colorful illustrations of a prolapsed rectum. At the time she ordered the book she said she was getting it from a new clinic in Minnesota, and it must have been the Mayo Clinic.

Our lives on the farm were basic with only the bare necessities in regards to home furnishings and farm equipment. We had no electricity, no indoor plumbing and no tractor to light the labor load. Everything depended on human strength and the strength of our animals.

Survival on a farm in Rural America in the 1930's was akin to survival in the wilds, depending on wit and know how. Seldom was there a cry for help without first deciding if the situation could be handled alone. The treatment of illness was approached in the same fashion.

I am thankful for the perseverance and fortitude I learned from my parents and grandparents.

Chapter Fifteen

The Games We Played

Needless to say we didn't have toys. I remember a doll for me and a dump truck for Dennis while we were still quite young. We had a few marbles and I had a little blue telephone once. I had a bisque doll that my grandmother Moore gave me. She was very fragile and I ended up breaking her moveable arms and legs. She was a little-girl doll. Later when we were older Dad bought a bicycle for me and a pony for Dennis. We didn't miss toys since you can't miss something you never have.

Mom made a large rag doll for me which was about three feet tall. We made a lot of our own toys such as hickory limb whistles and sling shots. One time I made a checker board and we used buttons for the pieces.

Harold Glenn taught us how to make hickory whistles. He would saunter through the woods until he came to a hickory limb that was just right, and cut it from the tree. Then we would all sit on the ground while Harold went to work whittling. He would cut a piece of the limb about six or eight inches long and then rub it to make the bark turn loose. He showed us how we could get different sounds by using different sized limbs and cutting them different. Some day I want to demonstrate this craft to my grandchildren.

One day we found some pieces of broken window pane lying in a little pile under the house. We proceeded to look through the broken edges by turning the glass sideways. We squinted and looked, looked and squinted and made our eyes hurt from strain but it was wonderful, the marvelous things we saw through the broken edges. There were linings of coffins, flowers, whatever our imagination was willing to conjure up.

When Dennis and I were quite small I remember Mom playing "Hide the Thimble" with us at night. She would hide the thimble and Dennis and I would look for it. We also played a game called "Come to Supper" but I don't remember anything else about the game.

Mom loved to read murder mysteries and she began reading them to us at night while Dad was at work. I remember how scary some of them were. When Dad found out about her reading them to us he told her he didn't think it was a good idea, so she never read them to us again.

One morning Mom called me and asked me to get up. I wondered why she would be getting me up but when I sat up I saw a bright blue bicycle parked at the foot of my bed. Dad had bought it from a man at the mines and pushed it home for me. What a wonderful surprise.

I learned how to patch the inner tubes for my bicycle and change the tires and put the sprocket chain back on when it came off.

There was always bailing wire around on the farm so if we needed some to repair something we could feel free to use it. It was amazing how it would get hot when we bent it for a few minutes and then it would break in two.

One of the things we would do in the summer was to climb small trees and sway them over and get off. Some of the trees wouldn't bend, so often we would have to try two or more trees before we got one that was just right. When we found one that seemed right we would begin swaying it back and forth. We would sway it back and forth until we could get it to bend to the ground so we could jump off. What a thrill this was.

Another thing we would do was crawl into a metal barrel and roll down a hill. The first few times we did this our bodies were banged and bruised so we gathered dead grass and padded the barrel on three sides where we placed our bodies so we would have fewer bumps. We would have to place our legs in such a manner where we could all lie down in the barrel and have enough room. It was a tight fit. To get the barrel started rolling we would sway our bodies from side to side and eventually it would start rolling.

We rolled down a hill that had recently been cleared and the stumps would hamper our journey. When we hit a stump it would shift how the barrel would continue its roll. This was a lot of fun. We only did this one winter, because we got too big to all fit into the barrel.

Chain Gang

We were always looking for something new and different to do in our playing. One time we decided we would play as if we were a part of a chain gang. Don't ask me how we knew about chain gangs. We lived far out in the country and never came in contact with prisoners or chain gangs. Nevertheless we found three chains and fastened them to our ankles. Everywhere we went we drug the chains. We played this way for several days until a man came along and saw us. He asked what we were doing. We told him we were playing like we were part of a chain gang. He said to me. "Does your mother know you are playing this game? A pretty little girl like you should not be playing such a game." I took the chain off right then and threw it away. We never played that game again.

Lightening bugs

Summertime was a great time for children in the country. The sky was lit up with lightening bugs and we would catch them and put them in a fruit jar. There were so many more then than there are now.

Also we were fascinated by the jar fly skeletons that would be lying around. Once in a while we would catch one that was still alive and put a string around his neck and watch him fly around.

The Murdered Turtle

One day Harold, Dennis and I were traipsing through a wooded area where a small creek was running through the bamboo and under brush. We spotted a large snapping turtle and we caught it and played with it for a while by examining his skin on the folds of his neck and turned him upside down and examined his underside. While we were pulling and tugging on him he was very patient and didn't put up a fuss.

We talked about making turtle soup or taking him back to the house and keeping him as a pet. Finally I said "Lets kill him." Harold said, "You don't want to do that, Jewell."

But I was adamant about it so Harold took out his pocket knife and began stabbing him. He eventually died and we cut his beautiful shell off his back and threw it up on the bank.

We decided to wait until it dried out and we would come back and get it.

Sometime later I asked Harold if he ever went back down to the creek and got the shell and he lowered his head and quietly said. "No."

Celtic Puzzles

Harold also taught us how to draw a Celtic puzzle. He would make 16 dots spaced at equal distances apart on a piece of paper and then connect the dots making a beautiful design. (See below) Dennis learned how to draw the design before I did but eventually I learned as well.

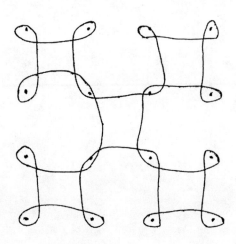

Chapter Sixteen

Pet Crows

One summer Dad came to the house and told Dennis and me about a crow's nest that was fairly close to the ground.

So Dennis and I set out for the tree. We had trouble finding the tree and climbed up several tall trees which contained squirrel nests.

We went back to the house and told him we couldn't find the crows nest but told him about climbing the tall trees and looking into the squirrels nest. He told us exactly where the crows nest was and told us not to climb any more tall trees since we might fall.

The second time we found the crows nest and brought back the three little crows to the house. We fed them chicken feed moistened and rolled up into balls. We would stand over the crows and say, "Caw, caw." They would open their mouths wide and we would drop the balls into their mouths.

The crows thrived and became quite large. One day during a storm they all few away and we never saw them again.

Chapter Seventeen

Neighbors

Our neighbors were scattered. Uncle Guthrie, Aunt Augusta and Harold Glenn, lived west of us down a hill and upon another smaller hill. The Flynn House was to the south of us. To the north were several houses closer together.

One of the houses to the northwest of us was rented. We never did know any of the people who lived there except the little boy. He was a small child probably five or six years of age. One day he came to see us and he had a quarter that he kept fondling in his hand. He told us that his mother's boy friend had given it to him to leave the house for a while so he decided to come and see us. That was the only time we saw the little boy and the family moved shortly thereafter.

Also to the north of us was where Aunt Augusta's father, Mr. Hughes lived. I don't remember much about the place except the barnyard. They had a huge tree hollowed out for a watering trough. It was the biggest tree I ever saw. The trough was long and a spring ran into it. I remember it being very cool under the trees around the trough.

I remember Mr. Hughes had a bull which he kept locked up on the barn. One day Harold, Dennis and I went to the barn and started teasing the bull and got him riled up. Mr. Hughes yelled at us when he found out what we were up to.

The Hughes had one boy that was single and still living at home. His name was Johnny. Johnny had met a girl in town with the name of Mary. He was really in love. One day he was cultivating a field and sitting on the iron seat of the cultivator.

Every time he would rise up we saw there was a hole in his pants and we could see a small portion of his bottom. He had on no underwear. I thought then it must be wonderful to be so in love that you don't even know when you have a hole in your pants.

In the direction of the Hughes House was where Aunt Vada and Uncle T. C Belmar lived for a short time. Dennis and I went down there one time since Aunt Vada had told us we could go walking in the woods, but when we got there we couldn't go since the wind was blowing so hard a tree might blow over on us. I remember how disappointed I was.

One of their little girls had a large stomach and Mom said she probably had worms. Their oldest girl was named Martha Ulee and we slept together one night. She reached over and got my hand and placed it between her legs. I immediately pulled it away and she did the same thing again. I pulled it back a second time and that was the end of it.

Aunt Vada and Uncle T. C. didn't live there very long and I never saw them again. Aunt Vada kept having children and finally died during the sixth or seventh pregnancy of kidney poisoning.

We had another family living East of us. The man was a mining manager or something to do with the mines. I remember Dad went over to their house and played cards a few times.

Another neighbor had three grown daughters and two grown sons living at home. One daughter had an illegitimate son and the other two girls were working towards that goal. On Saturday afternoons the two girls, without children, would stand on the street corner wearing evening dresses. I asked Mom why they were dressed that way and she said, "They are trying to catch a man."

The father would haul the two sons home from town in his farm wagon. They would lie in the back unconscious from too much drink. The man was a carpenter and didn't have to buy feed but he hauled his sons like bags of feed.

One summer afternoon a neighbor woman by the name of "Arnie", her two children, mom, Dennis and I went swimming in the creek. We enjoyed swimming for quite sometime when Arnie started screaming and kicking and splashing trying to get out of the water. She screamed, "There is a snake wrapped around my leg." She lifted her leg up out of the water and for sure there was a snake wrapped around it. I was sitting on the bank and saw it with my own eyes. That finished the swimming.

Our neighbors were country people and all worked hard and long in the fields, in their homes or whatever there was to do. They were all kind to me and I felt loved when I was with them.

Chapter Eighteen
The Flynn House

There was a farm house near our home that was closed with all the furnishings still in it. Both the farmer and his wife had died and their family let it stand for a while. One summer they decided to sell it as an estate sale including all the furnishings. Dad bought some leather harness and Mom bought an antique lamp. The harness had been hanging in the barn for several years and was dry rotted and when Dad tried to use it the harness fell to pieces. He would fasten the leather tracers back together with bailing wire which would work for a while. Finally he had so many patched places he gave up on ever using the harness again.

The antique lamp didn't last long either. Mom, Dennis and I were locked out of the house one day and Mom broke out the window pane. She lifted Dennis up into the window so he could go around and open the door. When she lifted him up into the window and he got into the house he pushed over the table which held the antique lamp and it fell to the floor smashing into many pieces. Mom said, "There went my lamp."

It would be several days before we went back to town so Mom put a piece of cardboard on the window where she had broken the pane. We had a goat that ate everything in sight so he chewed off the cardboard. Mom always came up with another piece of cardboard to cover the window.

Now that the house was sold we had new neighbors. The first family who lived there was a cousin of Dad's by the name of Hester Holloman and his wife and little girl. It was a large house and they didn't use all the rooms and used one room for storage. In the storage room they had a gas mask that Mr. Holloman had used during the First World War. It was a gruesome looking thing and I did not go into the room any more since the mask was frightening to me.

Mr. Holloman was suffering from shell shock from the war and was very nervous. He would tremble when he was uneasy about something. He took a job in the mines with Dad and had to go underground. Dad said the men cautioned him about how to step and how to hold when in the mines. In spite of all their cautioning one day he fell to his death. They had not lived in the house very long.

The next family who lived in the Flynn house was a woman and several children. The father worked in town and came home on the weekends. The mother was very pretty but her beauty was fading. She would sit at her dressing table for hours getting ready for her husband to come home and take her out on Saturday night.

The oldest child was a girl about twelve or so. The mother would send her oldest girl to the mail box beside the road and wait for the mailman to come. One day it was snowing and I saw the girl standing waiting for the mailman in the snow with open toed shoes. She had on a sweatshirt that had been made into a jacket and no warm top coat. I just looked at her wondering how long she would have to wait. The mailman always ran late when the weather was bad.

One day the next summer when I was going by their house the girl showed me a new car that belonged to someone who was visiting them. The car was brand new and had folding down seats that would make a bed. We found out later that the car was stolen.

That family didn't live there very long either.

Chapter Nineteen

Trips to Town

We always looked forward to our trips to town. We never bought anything much except the customary ice cream cone. The ice cream would always be two scoops of vanilla and we would savor every bite. Harold always got ice cream when he went to town too. Then one day I asked Harold if he still got an ice cream cone when he went to town and he said "No, I got tired of people watching me eat it."

We would get only one pack of Juicy Fruit gum and it would have to last us until the next time to town.

One day Mom was standing and talking to our neighbor that had a bastard son and the boy kept rubbing his snotty nose on her coat. She kept trying to get him to stop but to no avail. While they were talking I was standing by and chewing the last piece of gum we had. Dennis said, "Jewell, let me chew that gum for a while." I took the gum from my mouth and handed to Dennis who immediately started chewing it. Mom screamed, "Jewell, don't do that. Haven't you ever heard of germs?"

We never got anything much when we went to town, but I spied a toy phone that I wanted a lot and Mom bought it for me.

I think what interested me the most was watching the horses hold the wagon back when going down a hill. They would hunker down and bow their back legs to hold the wagon back to keep the wagon from running into them.

Chapter Twenty

Our Animals

The animals on our farm consisted of three or four milk cows, three or four horses, once-in-a-while a goat or two, chickens, hogs, two dogs and cats. For a few years my brother, Dennis, had a Shetland pony.

All animals were expected to be of some value or usefulness. For instance, one of our dogs was a black bulldog and the other one was a black and white long-hair similar to a border collie. The bulldog was called "Old Black" and the smaller dog was called "Skippy." Old Black was taught to pull our water in a small cart up the hill from the spring. Most days he was only required to pull one or two loads up the hill but on wash day he made many trips.

Dennis made a cart from a dynamite box on two wheels which was just large enough to hold two one-gallon buckets of water. He pieced together a harness from old hame strings, a few brads and bailing wire. Old Black paid his way in hard work but Skippy wasn't much good for anything except once in a while during summer he would help Old Black kill snakes. The dogs would grab the snake in their mouths and sling them from side to side until they disintegrated. One time we came up on two black snakes and Skippy realized he had one all to himself so he came through and both snakes were killed.

Skippy was a sneaky dog. He would walk around with his head down as if he were afraid of something or up to no good. Daddy couldn't stand that dog. Old Black always stood erect with his square shoulders bulging as if he was waiting to take on the world. He was a powerhouse of a dog.

When Daddy discovered that Skippy was sucking eggs he decided that it was time for the dog to go. The useless dog was eating up our profits.

One day at school one of my schoolmates said that she would like to have a dog so being the Good Samaritan that I am, I told her about Skippy, but not quite all. She said she would ask her mother that night and let me know the next day. So the next day she said she would walk home with me to pick up the dog. On our way from school to my house we were walking along talking about what I do not know except we started talking about her future dog. I was prattling along like a seven-year-old and by this time I must have realized that I really didn't want to part with Skippy so I said something to the effect that he sucked eggs. My past friend stopped walking and said, "He sucks eggs? Mamma doesn't want a dog that sucks eggs." She then said she would go on back home and tell her mother the latest development and let me know the next day at school. The next day she reported that they didn't want the dog.

Daddy offered the dog to all the neighbors, but none of them wanted Skippy either, so he came up with another plan. He asked my Uncle Guthrie to take the dog out into the woods and kill him. For some reason Dad didn't want to do it himself. Uncle Guthrie came by the house carrying a rope for a leash to pick up the dog and do the deed. Leading Skippy he walked into the woods. Sometime later he came sauntering back with Skippy trotting along beside him. With a sheepish smile on his face he remarked, "I couldn't do it." The dog practically beat him back to the house.

To this day I don't know what happened to Skippy. I do know we didn't move him with us to Illinois. I was too young to keep up with everything. Perhaps Dad found a home for him with one of the neighbors in Crittenden County or he might have done the deed himself.

Bull dogs had shady reputations and for some reason one of the neighbors complained about Old Black so we had to keep him tied up. One morning we got up and he was gone carrying part of his rope with him. For few days he didn't return and we had no idea what happened to him. A day or two later we heard a dog barking far off in the woods. This went on for two or three days and then Daddy said, "I am going over there and check that barking out to see if it might be Old Black," Sure enough it was Old Black and Daddy was beaming when he brought him back to the house.

We didn't honor our farm animals with names unless they were pets as the dogs were or I had a cat once that I called "Shirley." The horses were referred to as the "Old Mare," or the "Old Roan." The cows were referred top as that "Old Black Cow" or that "Old Horned Cow." The animals were identified by their characteristics or nature as mean or sneaky. (Several years later when I learned that my husband's family called their milk cow "Joanne" I found it very strange.) Dennis called his pony "Old Barney."

I had a bike that I really loved but Dennis said he wanted a pony since "you don't have to push a pony uphill." So Dad purchased a black Shetland pony for Dennis.

One day in early spring all the farmers in the valley were out plowing, Daddy included, and our dapple-gray mare fell in a deep ditch on her back with her feet flailing in the air. It was impossible for her to get up. The ditch was narrow and came to a "v" at the bottom. Daddy asked the other farmers to look the situation over to determine if she could be rescued. The farmers stood at the top of the ravine and looked at the helpless mare struggling in the ditch and it was apparent if she wasn't helped she would wear herself out and possibly die. The decision was made to put ropes around her body and pull her out. We children were told to get out of the way so I didn't see the actual rescue. The mare was pulled from the ravine and the next time I saw her she was standing in the pasture with her head down as if she was trying to determine if she was all right. I don't remember anything about the mare after that or how long she was a part of our farm population. Daddy was always trading livestock and our animals came and went.

If an animal was difficult to handle it was not with us very long. Dad bought a mule one time to pull the small wagon which Mom used to go to town for groceries. The mule had the common trait of balking but in addition to that habit, he kicked. When he kicked the front end out of the wagon, Dad decided it was time to let him go.

Dennis' Shetland pony was very contrary and we didn't have him very long either.

One day I started to ride Barney and when I got on him I had my boots in my hands and I must have touched his neck with the boots and frightened him, because he took off running as fast as he could. I sawed the reins as hard as I could but he wouldn't stop. I finally decided to jump off and landed in a pile of rocks skinning my knees and hands. Dennis was nearby so he caught Barney and got on him saying, "You want to run. Let's run." He rode him up and down the field as fast as he could and exhausted him.

It seems we didn't have Barney much longer than that and I don't remember ever trying to ride him again. He was a stubborn small animal and Dennis probably outgrew him.

When I became old enough I was put to milking and Mom and I would milk in the evening. Daddy was probably working the evening shift at the mines. Dad had built a high rail fence around a lot along one side of the barn where we would put the cows at milking time. The cows would be fed and while they were eating we would milk. Mom assigned me a "big-ole" cow with long horns to milk and while I was tugging at her teats she kept switching her tail and was very restless and then turned and started chasing me. I remember seeing those long horns coming at me and, terrified, I ran and got on top of the rail fence. The first thing Mom asked was if I had long fingernails. Since I bit my nails all the time it is doubtful I had long nails. She finished the milking.

One morning when we went to the barn to do the milking we found a new calf. When I asked Mom where the calf came from she told me the cow dug it up. While Mom was milking I was going around trying to find a place where I thought the cow could have dug up the calf. I finally found a soft place in the floor of the barn and told Mom, "This is probably the place where she dug the calf up because it is soft here." Mom just looked at me with no comment.

The barn was actually an old abandoned house with some of the wooden floors still in tact. In the front room of the house an old surrey was stored. There was a big room in the middle that was still floored so that is where Dad put the hay on one side and corn in the other. One fall when Dad put the corn in the barn we had an onslaught of huge rats. A neighbor had several half-grown cats that he gave to

Dad to kill the rats. Dad got the cats from the neighbor one afternoon and the next morning when we went over to the barn all the cats were lying around the barn with their heads chewed off. The rats killed the cats. I don't know what the next step was in combating the rats.

It seems one summer the snakes were prolific. Mom, Dennis and I were walking in the pasture one day and we came up on a brown snake. The dogs were with us as always. Mom struck the snake with a stick and his narrow head spread wide. It was really strange looking. His head was about the size of a saucer. Mom said later that she was sorry she didn't try to capture the snake and turn it over to the proper organization since she had never before heard of an adder in Kentucky.

One winter the farmers fattened hogs to see who could raise the biggest and fattest. So, of course, Dad had to get in on the competition. He built a pen up behind the house, convenient for feeding, which was just large enough for one hog and chose the best of the litter. He put the hog in the pen and Mom and Dad fed it unmercifully. The hog gained so much weight his body stretched from one corner of the pen to the other. He was huge and the farmers guessed his weight as being around 1200 pounds. All the neighbors came when Dad decided it was time to butcher the hog. After all the butchering, slicing, and rendering were done, Dad and Mom decided the whole thing had been a complete waste of time and money. There was not much usable meat and all they netted from the endeavor were many cans of lard.

One of the men who came and helped with the butchering had been bitten by a rabid dog a few years earlier. He had the series of shots for the disease. He had trouble straightening up and bent over when he carried the slabs of meat. He trembled terribly and could hardly hold a cup of coffee. He told us that he wished he hadn't had the shots and just gone ahead and died since the side effects of the shots had been so severe.

If our animals were gentle and did the work they were supposed to do Dad honored them by keeping them in our farm population for many years.

Dad's milk cows were Jerseys which at the time were considered good milk producers. He then purchased some Guernsey, which were larger in stature and was also fairly good milk producers. There was always talk about upgrading the herd but the expense of a good bull prohibited his proceeding with his plan. However, he saved his money and in due time he had enough to purchase a bull. The price was within Dad's means so the deal was closed. Dad and Mom decided they could walk the bull across the fields since he purchased the bull from a neighbor who was only two farms over from ours. There weren't fences at that time so they could walk him through the fields and not have to take him onto the road. The weather was sunny and Dad and Mom started out one afternoon to lead the bull home. They were able to get him in a neighbor's field next to our farm but the bull balked and would not go any further. For three days they worked and prodded the bull trying to get him to our barn. He would not budge out of his tracks. Dad tried whipping him but to no avail. They came back to the house on the second day exhausted and puzzled as to how they could get him home. On the third day they came back to the house and when I asked Mom if they got the bull home, she smiled and said, "No. We beat him to death." In my young mind I could not comprehend how such a thing could happen and why Mom could smile at such a loss. Dad had saved for months to get enough money to buy the bull. How could he kill him? The bull was never mentioned again and never again did Dad attempt to get enough money together to buy another one. Through the years I have reasoned that Dad must have been extremely disappointed and from pure desperation, he beat the stubborn animal to death.

This must have been the time that we saw the rabid dog. Mom had told us about how the rabid dog would foam around his mouth and would try to bite anything in his path. Dennis and I were at the house alone and I was looking out the window. I saw a slobbering dog coming across the yard. He was snapping at the chickens. I called Dennis and told him to come into the house since I thought that was a mad dog. Dennis came into the house and we stood at the window and watched the dog disappear down the road.

Dad's method of farming was archaic. He still plowed with a single bladed plow with a team consisting of two horses. One time he heard a program on our battery powered radio that they were having a mule day in some town in Tennessee and he decided he could really speed up his farming process if he had a span of good mules.

He ordered some brochures from a place in Tennessee and the material was fascinating. There were large black and white glossy pictures of mules and Dad spent a great deal of time dreaming, but that was all there was to it, since he eventually gave up on his dream with the realization that he could not afford the mules. This was during the time when some of the farmers were dreaming of tractors but Dad would have been happy with a span of mules.

In the days before modernization on the farms everything was more personal and we were more aware of our surroundings and the traits of our animals.

In looking back on our life on the farm I realize that the animals we did not have or never could have afforded affected our lives almost as much as the ones we did have.

Chapter Twenty One

Our First Radio

The highlight of our lives was when Dad came home with a table model radio and a battery for operating it. The battery was about twice the size of the radio. We would enjoy the radio until the battery ran down and then we would have to wait for a few weeks before we had the money for another one.

We enjoyed listening to the Grand Ole' Opry from Nashville and Mom listened to a soap opera called "The Guiding Light." The sponsor of the show was Lux Soap. I remember there was a character on the show called Neal and I couldn't quite understand the name. I kept thinking his name was "Nail."

In the evening I liked to listen to "Amos and Andy." One evening while Mom and Dad were at the barn milking I stayed at the house and did the supper dishes and listened to "Amos and Andy." It was their last broadcast and I cried when they went off. When Mom came back to the house she heard me crying and rushed into the house to see what was the matter. When I told her that "Amos and Andy" had gone off the air she just laughed at me.

Some of the time when I finished the dishes I would get two thimbles and from Mom's sewing basket, put the thimbles on two of my fingers and play a tune of the iron skillet.

Chapter Twenty Two

Dad's Calendars

(Published in *Reminisce* Magazine,
December and January 2008)

Earning a living in rural America during the 1930's was
the ultimate challenge for countless young farm families
and for those in Kentucky's Crittenden County, there
was no exception.

My parents were tenant farmers near the town of
Marion and once a month, Dad hitched the team of horses
to the farm wagon and went to town for supplies such as
groceries and livestock feed. Seldom were we stocked up on
everything.

Household staples were sold in bulk from barrels, with
each order weighed and measured. One time, Dad brought
home a 5-pound bag that was supposed to be sugar. When
Mom opened it, she discovered that the sugar was mixed
with salt, making it unusable.

The mix was discarded at a loss ill afforded from our meager grocery budget. We used sorghum on our oatmeal or grits until the next monthly trip to town.

On another occasion, Dad didn't get the writing tablet that was on Mom's list. She wrote often to my grandmother who lived in Southern Illinois, so she searched the house over trying to find a scrap of paper. Finally, she cut open a small brown paper bag and used that to write her letter.

Every winter, as soon as the new calendars appeared, Dad would get one from each of the stores at which he stopped and decide on the one that most suited his needs. The calendar had to be the full-page variety with at least a 2-inch-square box for each day.

In the late fall, Dad would make notes on the bottom of his current calendar in preparation for the next year's events—such as indicating when various farm animals were to have their young, births that were eagerly awaited. Once he got a new calendar, he transferred his notes and hung it on the living room wall for all to see.

The calendar was also used to record debts—which day of the month payments were due and the amounts of the payments. The original amount of each loan or purchase would be posted at the top of the calendar, along with the transaction date and balance due.

Dad loved to work with figures. He probably could have been a mathematician had he been able to go to school long enough to find out. My grandfather died when Dad was 16 years old, and a young man was more valuable in the fields than in the classroom.

It always amazed me how Dad could figure the amount of lumber needed for a project. At tree-harvest time, he'd walk through the woods, count the trees to be cut and observe their sizes. From this, he could project how much lumber the trees would produce.

I can't remember Dad ever having a new writing tool, holding short pencils in his gnarled hand to write and touching the lead to his tongue to moisten it so the writing would show up darker.

When his pencil needed sharpening, Dad took the ever-present pocket knife from his overalls pocket and whittled the pencil to sharpness, with just enough lead showing to write. The lead was usually lopsided and more square than round.

One time, Dad left his work at the sideboard. While he was away, I took his pencil, cut the wood down to show more lead and rubbed the lumpy lead on a piece of scraper to smooth it out. When Dad returned, I stood nearby to see if he noticed anything different. He asked me how I was able to smooth out the point and was pleased when I explained it to him.

In the long winter evenings my family would gather by the heating stove in the living room. My brother, Dennis, and I would do our home work, Mom would write letters and Dad would work on his calendars.

I remember fondly those days gone by, when we didn't have television and entertained ourselves by reading, playing games or working on improvised bookkeeping systems such as Dad's calendars.

Chapter Twenty Three
Mr. Grady, Our Mailman

The slogan "neither rain nor sleet or hail nor snow will prevent deliver of the mail" must have been penned by M. Grady our mailman in Crittenden County in the 1930's. Not only was he a faithful mailman but he apparently was a skillful driver of both the horse and buggy and the Model T. The weather predicted which vehicle he would use that day. On rainy days he would drive the buggy and make his stops with the buggy and horse dripping. Mr. Grady would look "drippy" except he was dry under the canopy of the buggy.

One day Mom had me wait for Mr. Grady and give him an order and the money for the items we were ordering. I waited for him and gave him the money and order. He placed the money and order in the seat beside him and I told him he didn't seal the envelope. He explained to me that he would have to purchase a money order with the money and then put the money order into the envelope before he would seal the envelope.

He later told Dad that I was a smart little girl since I noticed that he did not seal the envelope.

Later in life when I was visiting Marion, Kentucky, I learned that Mr. Grady had been made postmaster of the county. Good for him.

Chapter Twenty Four

Inconvenient Visitors

One summer a magazine salesman came through the neighborhood. He was carrying a colorful glossy magazine as a sample. Many of the women in the area bought a subscription and paid him. It was about lunch time when he got to our place so Mom gave him his lunch. She explained to him that she didn't have any money for the magazine so he said he would take one of the chickens that were running around in the yard. So shortly thereafter he left carrying one of Mom's old hens, going toward the little country store that was several miles from where we lived.

The magazines never came so the farm women had to admit they had been cheated.

Another time two men came by carrying shovels and stated they were looking for buried treasure and that according to a map they had that our yard was where it was buried. They asked if they could dig holes in our yard. Of course, they were given permission. I guess because Mom and Dad thought they could share anything that was dug up.

The men set to work and dug several holes in our back yard but to no avail. They were disappointed that they never found any treasure. One of the holes was dug fairly close to the back door and we had to walk around it. I don't know why the men weren't told to put the dirt back.

When it rained the holes would fill up with water and toads gathered in the hole closest to the kitchen door.

I loved playing with the toads and one day I had three in the house on the dining table. Mom came in and saw the toads jumping around on the table and yelled at me to take them outside. She said playing with the frogs was causing the warts on my hands. I still think frogs are adorable.

Chapter Twenty Five

Bits and Pieces

One day I was peeling boiled eggs and having a lot of trouble getting the shells to come off. Aunt Augusta was there and she told me to crack all the shell and then open the shell at the end where there is a hole in the egg. I tried it and it worked. To this day that is how I peel boiled eggs.

The sister of Aunt Augusta, Velma Margaret, lost her husband at a very early age. She had a little boy. I remember Velma cutting her husband's suits down and making suits for herself from them. He had two suits that she made over for herself.

One time Aunt Vada, Dad's sister, and her husband, T. C. Belmar, were visiting us.

Mom had gotten to where she would let me help with the biscuits. I was standing up in a chair patting out the biscuits. Mom would get the dough ready and let me pat them out. Aunt Vada yelled, "T.C. come in here and watch Jewell Evelyn pat out these biscuits. She doesn't even use a rolling pin. She pats them out by hand. That is something for a six year old."

One time we were playing outside close to the house where we had a metal rain barrel. It was a very cold morning and the barrel was covered with frost. I put my tongue to the barrel expecting to be able to lick some of the frost off. My tongue froze to the barrel. I stood there for a few seconds wondering what I could do. Finally I pulled my tongue free leaving a layer of skin. That was the first and only time I ever pursued to lick an object frozen.

One Christmas one of Dad's brothers, Uncle Jessie, came to visit us from Chicago where he had been working. He brought us a large box of assorted chocolates.

He opened it for us and sat me and Dennis down by the pot-bellied stove and with a smile on his face watched us munch on the chocolates. Looking back I don't remember offering Uncle Jessie any of the candy. We were so young that we hadn't learned any social graces.

Uncle Guthrie's cellar was something to behold. There were two kinds of apples, potatoes and turnips. I always like to go down there. We never ate anything however.

Chapter Twenty Six

Dad

Dad's farming was archaic using a single blade plow and everything depended on his brute strength and the strength of his team. He built a barn all by himself.

Not only did he farm but he worked during the winter months at a local fluorspar mines.

The only time he hired anyone to help him was when he had a special project such as clearing an area. He hired a black man to clear an area close to the house. It took him three or four days. He ate lunch with us at our table. He was a large man and kind. On the back of his head were many ridges. It was an interesting sight for a little six year old girl.

Mom boiled the dishes he ate from.

Dad also hired his brother-in-law, T. C. Belmar to do odd jobs around the place. One cold morning T. C. came by the house and was standing by the pot-bellied stove warming his hands and said it was so cold he hated to get out. Mom asked him to repeat what he said. She understood clearly what he said the first time and didn't like the sound of it. Daddy had gotten out early to walk to his job at the mines.

It wasn't long after that the Belmar's moved away.

During the winter months Dad would clean out the fence rows and repair the fences. The rows would look so nice when he had all the fences repaired and cleared of growth.

In the spring Dad would clean the manure out of the barn and put it on a field. It was in the fermenting stage and could not be put on the garden until it had cooled off. He hitched the team to a sledge and made many trips hauling the stinking stuff down to the field and spreading it.

He would haul matured manure from around the barn and spread it on the garden.

I remember one time Dad borrowed a dehorning device from one of the neighbors and cut the horns off our cows. It was a scary sight seeing the cows being tied up and their heads held and then have their horns cut off. Blood went everywhere. We kept the horns and played with them after they dried out.

One spring day when Dad started plowing a field that was quite a distance from the house, Mom went with him. This must have been before Dennis was born since I don't remember his being there. Mom took a large tin can and some coffee and water. She built a fire beside the field and cooked some coffee on the open fire. I remember the smell and I watched the coffee come to the top of the can and Mom would lift the can from the fire right before the coffee ran over.

Dad stopped plowing long enough to have a cup of coffee.

I liked to follow behind Dad in the furrow. I plopped my bare feet in the freshly plowed furrow on the cold moist ground behind Dad and the one-row plow and the bay team in front. It was a warm, sunny day and Dad was clucking to the team to keep it going at a steady pace. He was anxious to get the plowing done before it started raining.

There was a continuous crunch as the plow tore the earth and the roots popping, and the harness squeaking due to the pulling of the plow. I liked to watch the earth worms and the grubs pop out of the ground.

One summer day Dad plowed a field along a creek bottom for planting corn.

The next day when he went back to the field to continue preparing the ground for planting, there was a gaping hole about forty feet wide and several feet deep waiting for him where he had plowed the day before. Dad continued to work the field around the sink hole.

For many years I had bad dreams about the gaping hole and the sinking earth.

There were bamboo plants growing along the creek banks. They were such beautiful plants. The ridges at regular intervals along the trunks were fascinating to me.

Some times the wind would blow and dry out the land and trees. The leaves would turn up and show their lower sides which were lighter in color. The trees still do this today when there is a lot of wind. Mom would always say the trees were begging for water when their leaf bottoms were showing.

One spring we ordered 100 baby chickens and raised them in a corner of the living room. When they got big enough we turned them outside. When they were about half grown we ran out of chicken feed and they had to live on what they could find picking around the yard.

When Dad finally went to town and got some feed for them Mom fed them and they were so hungry one got choked and keeled over. It finally was able to swallow his large bite and got up and proceeded to eat.

One fall Mr. Neal Guess who was in charge of the bank in town ordered a load of wood. Dad worked for several days and finally got a load and delivered it to his house. His driveway was paved and was very steep and Dad said the horses had to really strain to get the load of wood up the driveway.

One night Dad was out with his brother, Lewis, and was traveling in Crane, Kentucky, when they witnessed an automobile accident where a sixteen year old girl was killed. He talked about the accident for days. One day I had on a dress that was green and white and black print and he said that was the color of the dress that the girl that was killed had on.

Dad had some of his school books and I loved them, especially the one about Indians.

When I was at the house alone I would always get the books out and look at the pictures. I would always forget to put them back and when Dad came home and saw his books out he would yell at Mom. I don't remember much about the books now except I think there was a math book, and English book and the one about Indians.

I don't know whatever happened to the books.

One winter the wood shingles on our house caught fire. Mom went out into the yard to go to the spring for some water and saw ashes falling. At first she thought it was snow but looked up and saw flames on the roof. Daddy happened to be home so she called him. He got a ladder and climbed up on the roof and proceeded to beat the fire out with a stick. He hit the roof several times and while he was striking the roof, he was yelling, "Fire, fire." But no one heard him because all the neighbors were too far away. He finally got the fire out and sawed and chopped more wooden shingles at the wood pile and repaired the roof.

Dad had a half sister, Audie, and an older half brother by the name of Jobie.

One fall about the time for Halloween we visited Aunt Audie at their farm which was in Francis, Kentucky. I remember they had a rambling house, a pond in front of their house and chickens running around in the yard. Aunt Audie gave me a piece of Halloween candy in the shape of a pumpkin. I had never seen candy like that before, however I took a bite out of it. When Mom saw that I had started eating it, she said, "You aren't going to eat it are you?"

Dad had many talents but I think his strength is what I appreciated the most. He would work all day at the mines and come home and hitch the team and go work in the fields until dark.

Chapter Twenty Seven

Me

At very early age, probably preschool, I had an imaginary friend, whom I called "Missus." I don't know where the name came from. Maybe from a story some one had read to me. Anyway my friend was my constant companion and I had many conversations with her. She was by my side in my playhouse and even when I went to bed.

I told Mom about my friend and she just looked at me as if she was trying to figure me out. She indicated that she did not approve of my imaginary friend or so I thought. My imaginary friend wasn't with me for long, probably until I started to school.

When I was very young I had some kind of nervous disorder where I would feel as if I would be holding a large object in my hand. The large object would be a rope or a large ball which would be so large I could hardly grasp it. The object would gradually get smaller and smaller until it would be as small as a hair in my hands. It was a weird and terrible sensation. Mom was afraid it was a form of epilepsy since her father was epileptic, but I think it was a residual effect of all those matches ate when I was eighteen months old. The sensation didn't happen very often and eventually it never came back.

One day Mom sent me over to one of our neighbors to buy some eggs. I guess our hens weren't laying or something. Anyway the neighbor had two little girls so I stayed quite a long time. It was so much fun being with the little girls. The woman said if I would wait a while for the hens to lay some more maybe they would have another egg or two that they could send.

I stayed a long time and decided I had better get back home. When I got home Mom asked me why I was gone so long and I told her we were waiting for the hens to lay more eggs.

That was the only time I went to that neighbors house, in spite of the fact that there were little girls to play with.

One day I was rambling around the yard and came across a large board which was about six by two foot that I decided would make a good table. I found four stakes and put the board down on the ground in a shady place and figured out where to drive the stakes in the ground for legs. After driving the stakes in the ground at the appropriate place I then placed the board on top and what a grand table. The board was weather beaten gray and was rather ragged at the ends but it made a beautiful table. I guess I was about six years old.

I gathered up fruit jar lids, broken dishes anything that I could find to stock my kitchen. Many hours were spent playing with my home-made table. But soon I learned that the sun shone on it most of the day. If I didn't get up early in the morning or go out there late in the afternoon when the sun was going down I didn't have much time playing at the table when it was in the shade. The sun would shine on the board and the edges would turn up so I would turn it over. It would be bowed in the middle for a few days but would eventually flatten out until the sun shone on it again and turned the edges of the board up again.

I eventually grew tired of having to continually turn my table top over so I got interested in something else and the board was eventually used for something else.

One day after a rain there was a nice mud puddle behind our house. I got an old pie pan and made a mud pie. I lined the pan with a thin layer of mud just like I had seen Mom line a pan with dough. I then formed small balls for berries and filled the pan with the "berries." Next I made a lattice top. What a masterpiece!!!! I was so proud of my pie that I took it into the kitchen and showed it to Mom and Dad who were sitting at the diner table. Mom said, "Oh, that looks good," as she dug her spoon into the pie for a bite. I yelled, "You ruined it."

One time I was sick and lying in bed by a window. I enjoyed looking out the window at the trees. I imagined I saw a woman up in the trees. It was such a clear vision that I called Mom and told her to look up into the tree and see her. Mom gave me a quizzical look and said she didn't see anything.

Another time Mom had supper ready and was waiting for Dad to come home. She told me to go out in front of the house and look down the road and see if he was coming.

The sun was going down so when I looked down at the foot of the hill the shadows looked just like a man on a horse and another man standing beside him. I went back into the house and told Mom that Daddy was standing down there talking to a man on a horse. She waited several minutes and then went out and looked down the road to see for herself.

She didn't see anything and came back and said I had lied. I don't remember whether or not Mom spanked me for telling the lie. In fact, I don't ever remember getting a spanking.

One time when Mom, Dennis and I were visiting my grandparents in Southern Illinois they were living at a place known as the "Place Between the Hills." Dennis and I decided to check out the hill on the right side of their place. We climbed to the top and looked down on the little farm. It was beautiful. When we started down the hill we decided to run. We started running and couldn't stop without falling. As we ran we just touched our feet to the ground to keep up our momentum. When we reached bottom both of us were in awe of the experience.

We stood there and looked back up at the hill where we had just come down and tried to make some sense of what had happened to us. I think it was a form of levitation. I will never know.

Back home, one day I looked out the back door and saw the preacher coming up the road with knee-high boots laced to his knees. I told Mom the preacher was coming "Just a bootlegging." When the preacher reached our door Mom told him what I had said. They both chuckled.

I don't know how old I was when I learned the real meaning of "bootlegging."

One late summer afternoon Harold, Dennis and I decided we wanted to go on a picnic. We made some peanut better and cracker sandwiches, put some water in a fruit jar and started walking. We went on the road toward my school and settled in some woods close to the road. I don't know why we didn't wait until we came to a grassy spot. We picked a soft spot in the woods with a lot of leaves. We were probably hungry so we settled down and started eating our lunch. Uncle Guthrie drove by in his car on his way to work and kicked up a lot of dust. That pretty well ended our picnic since the sandwiches didn't taste good with dust.

Uncle Guthrie apologized to us later but he didn't know we were so close to the road.

Uncle Guthrie had a one-seated car with a rumble seat. We loved to play in the car and Harold would show us how to shift the different gears. Uncle Guthrie put a stop to that real quick since he didn't like us playing in his car.

One day when I was very young, probably under four years of age, Mom and Dad toured the Eddyville State Prison during their opening house. My memory is not clear as to whom they went with. I only remember Mom telling me to play on the steps at the front of the building until they came back. I don't remember having a toy or anything to play with so I just jumped around on the steps until they came back.

I guess they figured I would be safe on the steps of a prison.

One night we were all in bed. Our beds were in the same great room which we called the "house." The kitchen was built as a lean-to at the back of the house. For some reason I touched my breast and I told Mom, "Mom, I just touched my breast nipple and there was a tingling feeling." There was only laughter from my parents.

One time when I was playing outside in the dirt I crammed some dirt up into my urethra and it immediately started burning unbearably. I started screaming and Mom came running to see what was wrong and when she found out what I had done, she got a wash pan of water that was always on a table in the kitchen and washed me thoroughly. The burning continued for several hours.

When I was still quite young I decided I would do the supper dishes. I was so short I couldn't reach the stove so I would push a chair up to the stove to stand on. Mom would put the dishpan on the stove and build a good fire in the stove to keep the dishwater hot. One evening I washed the supper dishes and continued to play in the dishwater. I loved to feel the suds since they were so soft. The stove had a roaring fire in it and the top on the stove was red. I wasn't paying attention to what I was doing so I put my spread palms down on the red hot stovetop. I didn't do the dishes for a while after that. Mom used her carbolic salves for my palms and they healed up without mishap.

Chapter Twenty Eight

Mom's Many Moods

One morning I came into the kitchen and said something to Mom. She replied, "Get the duck shit out of your eyes." I felt very badly about her mood and didn't know what duck shit was but I went and washed my face.

One time I said something about being unhappy and Mom replied, "You better be glad you aren't an orphan."

I remember one time I decided I was going to leave home. It was before I started to school. I started getting my things together and noticed that my slip needed to be washed so I washed my slip and hung it on the stove damper to dry. By the time my slip had dried I had forgotten about leaving.

One time Uncle T. C. Belmar drove Mom, Dennis and me to town. Dad was apparently working days at the mines. Dad gave Mom enough money to pay the bills. She paid all of them, she thought and had some money left over and used the money to buy some much needed pots and pans.

We were on the way home when she realized she had forgotten to save money for the handy man. She got really upset and said "Lockie is going to kill me." When she told Daddy what she had done, he said not to worry, it would be all right. He could pay him next payday.

Mom left Daddy many times and would go to my grandparent's home in Southern Illinois. She would cram our clothes into a pillow case and take off hiking. She would catch the mailman or anyone she could hitch a ride with. She always took Dennis and me with her.

Every time Mom left Daddy there was always trauma involved. She would be very upset. One time she had a little money and she bought herself a new dress. It was a wine crepe with pretty brass button. When she got home from my grandmother's house the dress was added to the pile in the closet.

When she got to my grandparents place she would talk about her plight in life. My grandmother would listen patiently and not say much. One time I heard Mom say something about being poor so I said "I am poor, see." as I pulled up my dress to show my stomach. Mom stated she wasn't talking about that kind of poor.

When Mom was happy she would sing as she worked around the farm. She had my cousin write down a long list of songs and she learned every one of them. She liked to sing "I'm leaving on that New River Train" and many church songs such as "I'll Fly Away."

There was an abandoned fluorspar mine close to our farm. We would pass it on our way to town and when we picked berries. Mom noticed that several pieces of spar lying on the ground near the mine. She decided she would pick it up and break off the rock and sell it.

She worked several weeks chipping the rock away from the spar. She bruised her hands many times working with the ore. She finally got enough to have it sold and called a trucking company to come and pick it up.

A neighbor boy told Dad he had put some spar on the pile so Daddy gave him part of the money that Mom had earned. No one had ever seen the boy working on the pile.

Daddy had an aunt by the name of Bell who wasn't right in the head. I don't know exactly what was wrong with her but they would tell about the way she would stand and pluck the spring on the screen door to make music. She was married to a prominent attorney so there couldn't have been much wrong with her. I don't recall ever seeing her. She died when I was preschool age. I only remember her funeral.

Mom never did like Daddy's family and she talked about them and Aunt Bell was no exception. On the day they were getting ready to go to her funeral Mom stood at the treadle sewing machine and hemmed a piece of cloth for a handkerchief. They were waiting for Uncle Guthrie to come by and pick them up. She posted me at the window and told me to watch him drive around the loop and then when he got to the barn to let her know. So I stood at the window and told her of his progress. I remember thinking to my self why she would cry about someone she didn't like?

One cold wintry day we all piled into Uncle Guthrie's car and went to visit my grandparents in Southern Illinois. Uncle Guthrie, Aunt Augusta, Dad and Mom rode in the front seat and Harold, Dennis and I rode in the rumble seat. Since it was a very cold day, while we were waiting for Uncle Guthrie and Aunt Augusta to come by and pick us up, Mom heated two bricks (all she had) and one large rock in the oven.

When they got there Mom wrapped the rock and bricks in newspaper and old blankets and put them on the floor of the car under the rumble seat to keep our feet warm. They must have worked since I don't remember getting cold sitting in the open rumble seat.

We had to cross the ferry at the Ohio River and we kids didn't have to get out of the car to see since we were already out in the open.

It was a fun trip and I don't recall us ever going together again. I guess we kids got too big to ride in the rumble seat.

We had a large sideboard that had become discolored so Mom decided she would refinish it. She stripped all the old varnish off and put on a new finish that was light oak. It turned orange and was ugly. She stripped it again and got some clear varnish that time. She stripped it two times and it had a lot of carvings on it. What patience. No job was too large for Mom.

One summer we had a tornado and it blew the kitchen door off its hinges and it landed in the yard.

Mom got a hammer and some nails and nailed it back together and put it back on the hinges. Mom was very adept with a hammer.

Mom decided she needed a closet so she got some lumber like the ceiling and made a closet in the corner of our living room. She did a marvelous job. It was straight and true. She put a top on it about eight feet up since our ceiling was 14 feet high. She never did get a rod in the closet and just put the clothes on the floor.

One time she was very upset about something and she went into the closet and sat on the pile of clothes and prayed and cried and cried.

When it came time for our cat to have her kittens she went into the closet and I remember her coming out of the closet meowing and biting her back side and then I saw a kitten coming out.

Mom made a pajama bag for me one time in the shape of a frog. She used green and yellow fabric. It was so cute and I would put it on my bed after I made it up.

In the winter Mom would piece quilts. She cut the pieces so close to the edge of the fabric that she ended up with a sack of nothing but small pieces of fabric. I remember how soft it was. It could have been used for a pillow.

She made a wedding ring quilt and another kind that I don't remember the name of the pattern.

She let me quilt a full size quilt. It was a simple affair from squares cut the same size and sewed together. I started out with all my squares being the same size but when I got to the end of the quilt the squares were about half the original size. It was a lopsided affair but we went ahead and lined and quilted it and used it for many years.

Finally when I was about 11, I was in seventh grade, Mom and Dad had a sale and sold all their livestock. They kept the horses. They decided to move to Southern Illinois across the road from Mom's parents' place.

I guess Dad decided if he moved Mom close to her parents she wouldn't be leaving him any more.

Dad bought twenty acres of land from the mining company and we had a house built. That lasted about a year, but that is another story.

When we were packing to move to Illinois Daddy cleaned the ground around the barn and house. He didn't leave any bent nails or pieces of scrap iron. He picked it all up and moved it with us.

Mom was an unfortunate woman and deserved much more from life than she received.

LaVergne, TN USA
18 November 2010
205429LV00001B/4/P